RIGHTEOUSNESS
INSIDE
OUT

RIGHTEOUSNESS INSIDE OUT

The Sermon on the Mount and the Radical Way of Jesus

MIKE COPE

LEAFWOOD
PUBLISHERS

Righteousness Inside Out
Published by Leafwood Publishers

Copyright 2003 by Mike Cope

ISBN 0-9728425-2-7
Printed in the United State of America

Cover design by *HisLight Designs*

Leafwood Publishers, Siloam Springs, AR
1-877-634-6004 toll free

03 04 05 06 07   9 8 7 6 5 4 3 2 1

DEDICATION

To

Matt and Christopher

and in memory of

Megan (1984-1994)

TABLE OF CONTENTS

Foreword
MAX LUCADO

et's say you have a car. And let's say that car is running poorly. Rather than having the purr of a kitten, it has the cough of a three-pack a day smoker. Rather than gliding down the road like a luxury liner, it yanks and jerks like a bull in a rodeo. Concerned, you chug into the mechanic's shop. You describe your problem and the mechanic confidently tells you to wait while he goes to get "just the thing" for your car.

He soon returns carrying—not pliers or gauges or a screwdriver—but a can of car wax. "What your car needs is a good wax job!" he exclaims. "Let me have an hour with her and she'll be shining like new."

That sounds a bit odd, but who are you to question? So you leave your car to the polishing mechanic.

An hour later you return. True to the mechanic's word, your car boasts a brilliant shine that it hasn't had in years. Enthused, you hop in. "Now, this car is gonna go!"

But go it doesn't. It shines, but it's still sluggish. It sparkles, but it's still slow.

Out comes the mechanic again. "I know the problem.

Let's paint it!" Again, trusting, you leave your ailing auto-
mobile with the mechanic who paints it fire-engine red.
You, again enthused, jump in the car only to find that,
though sparkling and freshly coated with paint, it still
stumbles like a drunk snail.

The well-meaning mechanic doesn't give up! He's
got all kinds of solutions to your car problems. New
roof. Whitewall tires. Fender guards. Fog lights. All add
zest to the outside, but nothing puts zip on the inside.

You're chuckling. You're wondering who would be
so silly to concentrate on the outside when everyone
knows the problem is on the inside?

Do you really want to know?

- A housewife battles with depression. Suggested solution by some misguided mechanic? Buy a new dress.

- A husband seeks advice for his marriage that is
  riding on the crest of a wave about to be slammed
  into the rocks. Suggested solution? Bail out!

- A dying church flounders like a fish on a beach.
  What can be done to bring life into the congregation? "Let's build a building!" someone suggests.

Case after case of treating the outside while ignoring
the inside. We polish the chrome and neglect the
engine. The housewife gets a new dress and her depression disappears! . . . for a day. Then the shadow returns.
The husband trades his wife in for a new model. The
result? Happiness! . . . for awhile, then the same personality traits that got him in trouble the first time go to
work again. The church meets proudly in its new facility
and the ranks swell with enthusiasm! . . . for a few
months. Then the flame flickers and dies, leaving a cold
church in a new building.

The exterior polished, the interior corroding. The

outside altered, the inside faltering. Cosmetic changes are only skin deep.

Perhaps that's why Jesus and the religious leaders were always singing different songs. The religious leaders thought an outside reformation would be sufficient. Jesus, however, took them to the heart of the problem, which was, and is, the problem of the heart.

Mike Cope, in the book you are about to read, does exactly the same. With skillful tools of scripture and script, he exposes the interior and diagnoses the problem. You, the reader, will be left with two options. You can take Mike's, or better said Christ's, counsel and fix the inside. Or you can chug-chug away, still outwardly sparkling but inwardly marking time until you explode.

Remember the point: The next time your spiritual walk sputters and spews, don't polish or paint; instead, penetrate. Go to the "Master Mechanic." It may well be time for an overhaul.

PREFACE

Jessica Cohen, a student at Yale, saw a classified ad in the *Yale Daily News*: "EGG DONOR NEEDED." The couple placing the ad was looking for an egg from just the right donor, and they were willing to pay handsomely for it. To the tune of $25,000.

They wanted the egg of an Ivy League college student—one who was over 5'5", of Jewish heritage, athletic, attractive, and with an SAT score of over 1500.

The fee caught her attention. She could use that twenty-five grand, she thought. So she started corresponding with the unnamed couple. And as she did, she was introduced to a whole world of online ads by similar couples. She located one site with 500 classifieds posted—what she called "an eBay for genetic material."

In addition to the ads from couples looking for eggs, there were promos from young women wanting to sell their eggs. "Hi! My name is Kimberly. I am 24 years old, 5'11" with blonde hair and green eyes. I previously donated eggs and the couple was blessed with BIG twin boys! The doctor told me I have perky ovaries! . . .

The doctor told me I had the most perfect eggs he had ever seen."

Cohen's e-mail correspondence with the anonymous husband was outrageous. This man and his wife expressed concern about her scores in math and science. Then the exchange came to a screeching halt when she finally e-mailed them some pictures of herself. His response came back: "I showed the pictures to [my wife] this AM. Personally, I think you look great. She said ho-hum."

In an essay in *Atlantic Monthly*, Cohen wondered what kind of bizarro world this was that she had entered. The answer is that it's a world that values the outside: looks, athletic ability, power, and wealth. It's a world that considers "gifted and talented" the student with a high IQ . . . rather than the one with compassion and courage.

The world into which Jesus came and spoke is very strange to us in many ways. But it's not as different a world as we might imagine. It was still a world where it was easier to define life—even religion!—by the externals.

Into this world, Jesus came speaking about another way of living—of living under the rule of God. Matthew boiled his message down to this: people should change their lives in view of the rule of God. "Repent, for the kingdom of heaven is near" (Matt. 4:17).

The Sermon on the Mount is an expansion of that theme. It clarifies what it means for a penitent person who's open to the reign of God to live.

The sanest piece of advice I've ever received about preaching came years ago from an older minister who suggested that every sermon should have at least one point. That seems obvious, but after delivering hundreds of sermons myself I can look back and wonder about a few of them: did they really have a point?

There is a clear point in this Sermon. The theme is righteousness, right living in light of the invasion of God's rule.

The world will pay top dollar for "accidents of birth," but Jesus is more concerned about the condition of one's heart. Instead of affirming the wealthy and power brokers, he announces God's blessing on the poor in spirit, the mourners, the meek, the hungry and thirsty, the merciful, the pure in heart, the peacemakers, and the persecuted.

His powerful words are not intended as impossible demands that drive us to our knees in need of grace (as Martin Luther believed). Rather, they begin in grace. God has entered this world and has offered his blessing. There is no works righteousness here. However, someone called into the rule of God by his mercy is also called into a new reality and into a new way of living.

It's inappropriate, according to Jesus, for someone to welcome the blessings of God without accepting the new life in God. At the end of the sermon he pictures someone crying out "Lord, Lord" while refusing to do the will of that Lord. God's response will be, in essence, "ho-hum." He isn't impressed with religious facade.

As you enter this study, please have your Bible and, much more importantly, your heart open. My hope is that you'll experience an increase in knowledge (information), a change of heart (formation), and a devotion to live differently (transformation).

Chapter I
GOD BLESS
THE CRAVERS

L arry is a friend and fellow scuba diver who, several years ago, was spearfishing ninety feet deep in the chilly Pacific waters near Catalina Island. With little air left in his tank and with his allowable bottom time for that depth almost gone, he spotted a fish that had "DINNER" written all over it.

With uncharacteristic disregard for safety, Larry began stalking the prey with his spear gun ready to fire. As he neared the fish and began aiming, however, he sucked on his regulator and got nothing. His air supply was gone! In ninety feet of ocean! With no dive buddy in view!

It took just a milli-second to decide what to do. Larry bolted toward the surface, slowly blowing out to keep his lungs from exploding. (The air in your lungs expands as pressure decreases when you ascend.)

At sixty feet he was hurting, at forty he was dizzy, at twenty he was on the verge of passing out. One thought dominated.

At that moment, he couldn't have cared less about the performance of the Dow Jones, about the next election, or about the upcoming baseball playoffs. He wasn't worried about L. A. traffic, about paying for his kids' college education, or about his need to shed a few pounds.

His laser focus was on one thing: air. Sweet, life-sustaining air.

So with one thread of conscious effort remaining, he pumped his thighs a few more times. Bursting to the surface, he gasped for breath. That was all he wanted. He wouldn't have traded that breath of air for every penny in Bill Gates' bank account.

Water, Water, Everywhere

Larry's predicament was too much water and too little air. Samuel Taylor Coleridge described the opposite crisis in "The Rime of the Ancient Mariner." The sailors were out in the midst of the ocean, and the wind had died. They were being punished for killing the albatross. Surrounded by fresh air, they were dying from lack of potable water.

There was no way without a breeze they could reach land, and as they were suffering they looked around at all the salt water:

> Water, water, everywhere,
> And all the boards did shrink;
> Water, water, everywhere,
> Nor any drop to drink.

Do you remember the story of Scott O'Grady, the Air Force fighter pilot who was gunned down over Bosnia while seeking to enforce the NATO no-fly zone? He survived for a week behind enemy lines, constantly battling dehydration. When his few packs of water were gone, he licked the drops of rain off of grass.

Then he relied on the moisture he was able to squeeze from his socks.

He likely was in the position of one of Jules Verne's characters from *A Journey to the Center of the Earth.* When they ran out of water and began craving that one thing, the character said, "I would have bartered a diamond mine for a glass of pure spring water."

Craving Happiness

Many people seem to crave happiness with that intensity. This obsession leads some to devote their lives to financial security. "If I could just find the right home, and if I could just pay off the SUV, and if I could just get the kids through college, and if I could beef up my retirement fund, then I'd be happy." Others search for happiness in sexual conquest, recreational drugs, religion, education, new relationships, or the fantasy world of television.

The pursuit of happiness has become so all-consuming in our society that Alexsandr Solzhenitsyn observed, "The meaning of life in the West has ceased to be seen as anything more lofty than 'the pursuit of happiness.'" Evidence that this would change after the terrorist attacks of September 11, 2001 was short lived. The hoped-for spiritual revival didn't happen; life just slowly returned to normal.

The ironic thing about happiness is that a "pursuit" is hardly the way to find it. People who pursue it, especially from the perspective of the American Dream, rarely find it.

Happiness is like sleep. You don't go to sleep by pursuing it. I remember a time my wife, Diane, was telling a friend (in my presence) about how disgustingly quick I can drop off to the land of lullaby. I'm like a two year old eating a potato chip, who falls asleep in the middle of eating it.

That night as I went to bed, I felt lucky. They had mentioned that it always took them fifteen to twenty minutes to fall asleep. So as I pulled up the sheet, I thought, "I am so fortunate to go to sleep so easily. How do I do it?" I lay there for hours thinking about how I go to sleep! (And after writing this paragraph and remembering that incident, it'll probably happen to me again tonight.) You don't go to sleep by concentrating on it.

Happiness is the same way. Genuine happiness comes as a serendipity. It is a by-product of a much greater pursuit. We need to crave something that is broader, deeper, and more significant than that.

Hungering for Righteousness

Jesus tells us the truth: the truly happy (blessed) people are those who hunger and thirst for righteousness. Note that he doesn't say, "Blessed are those who hunger and thirst for happiness." We can't set as our highest goal in life "to be happy," because that will only leave us frustrated. We're likely to destroy everything, everyone, and ourselves as we set out on such a quixotic quest.

Built into every person is an innate desire for something transcendent. We all want to touch and taste something lasting, something that goes beyond the here and now. That's what Jesus is speaking about! We long for something that doesn't erode with time, something that doesn't pale into insignificance, something that holds our lives together when tears and tragedy try to pull them apart.

So where do we turn in this longing for transcendence

in our lives? Listen to these testimonies of some God-hungry people:

As the deer pants for streams of water, so my soul pants for you, O God. My soul thirsts for God, for the living God. When can I go and meet with God?
Psalm 42

I am the bread of life. He who comes to me will never go hungry . . . .
Jesus, John 6:35

In him we live and move and have our being.
Paul, Acts 17:28

Thou hast made us for thine own, and our souls are restless until they rest in thee.
Augustine, *Confessions*

The word "righteousness" is used in different ways in the Bible. When Paul used it, for example, he was usually talking about something God declares you to be. Theologians use the term "forensic righteousness" to describe this divine work. In this sense, the word pretty well summarizes the redemptive work of God in Christ. We could never be morally right before God. We could never deserve anything good he might desire to give us, so he sent his own Son to die for us. "God made him who had no sin to be sin for us, so that in him we might become the righteousness of God" (2 Cor. 5:21).

Jesus used the term in a different sense in the Sermon on the Mount, however. There he was talking not so much about what God declares you to be as he was about what God is now making you into. We call this sanctification—the process of living lives commensurate with our belief that the rule of God has come in Christ. This "righteousness," then, is the inner life as it should be if filled with the love and truth of God.

This is where that craving for transcendence comes in. More than anything else, we must crave to be like God. And having seen God mostly clearly in his Son, we yearn to be conformed into his image. This is what the masterful sermon of Matthew 5-7 is telling us. In the words of Dallas Willard, the Sermon on the Mount is about "the sweet life of love and power, of truth and grace, that those who count on Jesus can even now lead in his kingdom . . . . His teachings illustrate how those alive in the kingdom can live, through the days and hours of their ordinary existence, on their way to the full world of God."[1]

Every Christ-follower ought to be passionate about this quest. We should never just float along, satisfied with our nice, mellow lives. This calls for intensity. For passion. For single-mindedness. Jesus had this in mind when he spoke of those who hunger and thirst for righteousness. They are focused on having the life of God formed within them. This is their constant dream—a dream that seizes their lives.

The Church Today

So how is the church today doing in the pursuit of righteousness? Is that single-mindedness evident? Do we find that kind of intensity in pursuing God of which Jesus spoke?

Why do we consume the latest mystery thriller while our Bibles collect dust on the shelf? Why do we convince ourselves that we're just "too busy" to participate in those actions which the church has historically undertaken in order to grow spiritually? Why do we lecture so much on prayer yet pray so little? Why do we sometimes give the impression that the true meaning of life is found in a job or some retirement fund—when Jesus plainly said it's found in hungering and thirsting for righteousness?

There's an interesting parallel in the "beatitude" of Psalm 1:

> Blessed is the man who does not walk in the counsel of the wicked or stand in the way of sinners or sit in the seat of mockers. But his delight is in the law of the Lord, and on his law he meditates day and night. He is like a tree planted by streams of water, which yields its fruit in season and whose leaf does not wither. Whatever he does prospers.

That's a picture of a person who craves righteousness, who longs to be like God. Such a person is still exposed to cold winters and hot summers, but they'll survive because their roots go down deep into the stream.

In a way, that's what Jesus was saying will be true of us when we crave holiness before God. Are we protected? No—at least there's no invisible shield around us to deflect all disappointments, illnesses, and temptations. We will still face those winters of tragedy and those summers of burned relationships. But we will survive!

When we lived on the coast of North Carolina, we experienced the powerful punch of Hurricane Diana, complete with seven hours of 110 mph winds. Between midnight and 7:00 a.m., we lost eight trees in our back yard. Each time one would fall with a crash, our two-year-old son, who was giddy with delight just to be allowed to stay up through the night, would squeal with delight: "Do it again, Daddy."

The morning light revealed the cause of death to our trees. They had life too easy! Growing right next to the coast, they enjoyed a high water table, meaning their roots barely dipped beneath the surface. With such a shallow root system, they were easy prey for a windbag like Diana.

By contrast, our West Texas mesquite trees would be much more likely to survive. Life isn't as cushy for them. They have to send roots to China to find water.

Those who build their life on the shallow pursuits of money, sex, prestige, and power are begging for a serious root canal! But those who sink their roots into a serious pursuit of God and godliness will endure with a tough, deep, peaceful joy.

Blessed are those who crave righteousness, Jesus said. Then his promise: they will be filled.

O God, be Thou exalted over my possessions. Nothing of earth's treasures small seem dear unto me if only Thou art glorified in my life. Be Thou exalted over my friendships. I am determined that Thou shalt be above all, though I must stand deserted and alone in the midst of the earth. Be Thou exalted above my comforts. Though it mean the loss of bodily comforts and the carrying of heavy crosses, I shall keep my vow made this day before Thee. Be Thou exalted over my reputation. Make me ambitious to please Thee even if as a result I must sink into obscurity and my name be forgotten as a dream. Rise, O Lord, into Thy proper place of honor, above my ambitions, above my likes and dislikes, above my family, my health and even my life itself. Let me decrease that Thou mayest increase; let me sink that Thou mayest rise above. Ride forth upon me as Thou didst ride into

Jerusalem mounted upon the humble little beast, a colt, the foal of an ass, and let me hear the children cry to Thee, "Hosanna in the highest."

—A. W. Tozer

Chapter 2
THE HEART OF
THE MATTER

For I tell you that unless your righteousness surpasses
that of the Pharisees and the teachers of the law, you
will certainly not enter the kingdom of heaven.
—Matthew 5:20

Behold, a certain woman purchased two identical Whirlpool freezers. Her husband, a devoted deer-hunter, had once again over-supplied the family. Early in her marriage she had objected to his obsession (which, of course, he called "a hobby"). She'd said something about "killing Bambi." But year after year, he continued to bring home more venison than she knew what to do with, so she finally caved and bought the freezers for the garage.

To avoid finding an extension cord, she plugged them into different electrical outlets in the garage, and filled both with the meat they'd picked up at the processors. Then off the family went for a two-week holiday break.

What she didn't realize was that one of the garage outlets had no juice. Seems they'd never actually used it since they moved into the house. So one of the freezers acted as a freezer; the other was just a storage shed.

In early January, they returned, the family hungry for venison steaks. She stood before the Whirlpool twins. They still looked just alike. Both were shiny and new. But, as she was about to find out, on the inside they were very different. Open one and smell it—fine! But open the other, take a whiff, and die right there! It's full of rottenness and decay.

Jesus warned that the Pharisees in his day were a lot like that freezer, looking just right on the outside, but rotten to the core inside.[1] The difference between his teaching and theirs was that he was focusing not just on the exterior actions of God's law but even more on the inner condition of the heart and character of a person. There is where the rule of God must begin!

Do not think that I have come to abolish the Law or the Prophets; I have not come to abolish them but to fulfill them. Truly I tell you, until heaven and earth disappear, not the smallest letter, not the least stroke of a pen, will by any means disappear from the Law until everything is accomplished. Anyone who sets aside one of the least of these commandments and teaches others accordingly will be called least in the kingdom of heaven, but whoever practices and teaches these commands will be called great in the kingdom of heaven. For I tell you that unless your righteousness surpasses that of the Pharisees and the teachers of the law, you will certainly not enter the kingdom of heaven.

Matt. 5:17-20

Matthew wants his church, who likely were Jewish Christians now in conflict with Jews who hadn't accepted Jesus as the Messiah,[2] to know that Jesus wasn't anti-law. Rather, Jesus would have viewed God's moral law as the writer of Psalm 119 did: "I delight in your commands because I love them" (v. 47). This wasn't the wearied, frazzled word of someone who'd been trying to be saved by law-keeping. Rather, it was the joyful word of a God-hungry person who'd been redeemed by God's mercy and who was thankful for his guidance and instruction.

Jesus didn't come to abolish the law and the prophets, but to fulfill them. He both showed (in his life) and taught how we might live the righteous life God had intended—a life where obedience flows naturally from redemption.

The Beatitudes had prepared for this paragraph. They offered God's blessing on the humble people—those will trust in God's power rather than in their own resources. They're willing to receive the kingdom. These are the ones who will be light in the world, shining before others so they may see such radically different lives and wind up praising the Father themselves.

Two Kinds of Righteousness

Now, in Matthew 5:17-20, we come to the central focus of the Sermon. Jesus says that our righteousness must surpass that of the teachers of the law and Pharisees. The rest of his message fleshes out what that looks like.

The remainder of chapter 5 offers six applications of this "new" righteousness. Each (5:21-26; 5:27-30; 5:31-32; 5:33-37; 5:38-42; and 5:43-48) comes with a contrast between what they'd heard and what he now says.

This is very important: What is Jesus contrasting? An old interpretation suggested that Jesus was laying a trump on top of Moses. "Moses was opposed to murder; I, however, am opposed to anger itself." According to this view, the gospel is an elevation of morality. The Old Testament was about external actions; the New Testament is about the heart. Formerly God was trying to control your deeds and your works, but now he seeks the heart and character of a person.

There are glaring problems with that interpretation, however. The most obvious one is that the same God is behind both testaments. The God who seeks the inner heart and character of Christ-followers sought the same from his people before Jesus lived. Immediately following the central confession of the Jewish faith—"Hear, O Israel: The Lord our God, the Lord is one"—the Israelites are instructed to "love the Lord your God with all your heart . . . ." (Deut. 6:4ff)

Marcion was an early heretic who said there were two different Gods. There was the Old Testament God: legalistic, angry, vindictive. This God sought only behavioral modification. Then came the God whom Jesus revealed, a God of love who wants both your actions and your heart.

But the early church recognized the horrific mistake behind Marcion's teaching. They understood that the same God who moved in the New Testament had also chosen Abraham and his descendants.

When Jesus contrasts what the people had heard about refraining from murder with his message about anger, he isn't going one up on Moses. Moses was speaking for the same God. It would be hard to read the Old Testament and believe that God really wasn't concerned about bitterness and rage!

Likewise, Jesus contrasts what they'd heard about adultery with his concern about lust. But didn't God care about lust in the Old Testament? Seriously now. Wasn't there a commandment that said something about coveting your neighbor's wife?

Jesus wasn't contrasting his way with Moses' way. Rather, he was contrasting his interpretation of Moses with a shallow, even perverted, interpretation of Moses. The choice, then, is between Jesus' way of looking at what God had always wanted and the Pharisee's reductionistic reading of the law.

That's what Jesus means when he calls for a "righteousness that surpasses that of the Pharisees and the teachers of the law." He's saying, in effect, "I want to lead you to what Moses was calling for long ago. This is what God is about."

Maybe Matthew had heard some charges being made about Jesus: "Aha! He's against the law! He's opposed to Moses!" So he makes sure we hear Jesus say, "I have not come to abolish the Law and the Prophets."

We sometimes talk about the two testaments in terms of radical discontinuity; but Jesus saw much continuity. He recognized the organic relationship between them. Does that mean we're under the covenant of Israel—that unique relationship God had with the physical descendants of Abraham? No. But the Old Testament is from God and is still instructive for God's people today. For from the beginning God was concerned with right living that must come from the inside out.

The problem with the influential religious leaders of the day was that they were often concerned only with behavior. They were like an apple that's shiny red on the outside. You grab it, your mouth begins to water, then you sink your teeth into it. But when you take that first bite, you discover that it's been eaten by worms on the inside.

Several years ago, Diane and I invited a university student over to our house for lunch after church. He told me, rather sheepishly, that he'd brought a date. (For students on a low-end budget, church is a great date!) I told him we'd love to have her as well.

Just before we gathered around our table to eat, I asked him to take his sports jacket off. (As I think about it, this really has been several years ago. I haven't seen a sports jacket on a student at church since . . . well, maybe since the Cowboys were a professional football team.) I'd already stripped my tie off and ditched my jacket.

The young man stammered, however, as if he didn't want to. I tried again to get him to relax a bit. So he got me off in a corner and said, reminding me of an old trick I knew well when I was in college, "The only part of my shirt I ironed was my cuffs and the collar." He had pressed just the part that showed. The rest of the shirt looked like he'd ironed it with a weedeater!

That was the Pharisees: the part people could see looked great, but a weedeater appeared to have done the ironing on the inside.

The sermon in Matthew 5-7 calls us to become something different. The Pharisees wanted more obedience; Jesus wanted deeper obedience. So while they were adding law upon law and prohibition upon prohibition, he was calling for heart surgery.

The Radical Difference

As you read through Matthew's gospel, some of the differences between Jesus and the religious leaders begin to emerge.

It's clear, for example, that they had a different motive. "Everything they do," Jesus warned, "is done for people to see" (23:5). They wanted to be thought of as honest people; you just couldn't necessarily count on them to be honest (5:33-37; 23:16-22). We call that gap between appearance and inner reality "hypocrisy." No wonder, then, Jesus condemns them with these words again and again: "Woe to you, teachers of the law and Pharisees, you hypocrites!" (23:13, 15, 23, 25, 27, 29).

T. S. Eliot, in "Murder in the Cathedral," has three tempters coming to Thomas Becket, trying to get him to do something awe-inspiring in order to receive power and prestige. Becket doesn't succumb to those temptations, however. But then an unexpected guest, a fourth tempter, comes in. And this tempter goes to the heart of the matter when he says, "You need to be martyred as you are about to be anyway, but do it for glory." It's the right action, but the wrong motives. Then the tempter continues, "Saint and martyr rule from the tomb." Your enemies will worry about you coming back to haunt them, he promises. Pilgrims will line up at your grave.

Then comes Eliot's famous lines, "The last temptation is the greatest treason. To do the right deed for the wrong reason."

So it was with the Pharisees. Lots of right actions, but also wrong motives. If we miss this emphasis, we end up with hundreds of good, reliable church people who will be at every service, who may teach a class when called upon, who will give something for the annual missions collection—but who are as spiritually shallow as a baby's wading pool.

Such people have had nothing happen on the inside. They're as shallow twenty years after coming to Christ as they were the day they were reborn. You hear it in the sour attitudes and the gossip; you see it in the bitterness and the explosive anger.

Another difference was that the religious leaders

concentrated on different issues. What were the Pharisees' headline issues?

In Matthew 12, Jesus was busy healing and feeding, yet their big concern was grain plucking. They challenged him, "Look! Your disciples are doing what is unlawful on the Sabbath." Amazing Grain—their favorite topic!

Later in the gospel, the Pharisees and scribes were concerned about the washing of hands. Jesus underscored their hypocrisy and misplaced values by saying, in essence, "You've made a mockery of something really important: the commandment to honor your father and mother. You find a way around that explicit command of God. You're big on hand-washing, but you fail to keep the fifth commandment."[3] Even later he chided them:

> *You're hopeless, you religion scholars and Pharisees! Frauds! You keep meticulous account books, tithing on every nickel and dime you get, but on the meat of God's Law, things like fairness and compassion and commitment—the absolute basics!—you carelessly take it or leave it. Careful bookkeeping is commendable, but the basics are required. Do you have any idea how silly you look, writing a life story that's wrong from start to finish, nitpicking over commas and semicolons?*
> Matt. 23:23-24, The Message

A third major difference between Jesus and the religious leaders was in character. The Pharisees were intent on the outward expression of religion. They were active in doing but were missing the inner desire to be God's person in both thought and behavior. His chiding continues in Matthew 23 (highlighted again by Eugene Peterson's translation):

> *You're hopeless, you religion scholars and Pharisees! Frauds! You burnish the surface of your cups and bowls*

*so they sparkle in the sun, while the insides are
maggoty with your greed and gluttony. Stupid Pharisee!
Scour the insides, and then the gleaming surface will
mean something.*

*You're hopeless, you religion scholars and Pharisees!
Frauds! You're like manicured grave plots, grass clipped
and the flowers bright, but six feet down it's all rotting
bones and worm-eaten flesh. People look at you and
think you're saints, but beneath the skin you're total
frauds.*

Matt. 23:25-28, The Message

Read the Beatitudes carefully. They depict the opposite kind of person from how the religious leaders are
portrayed by Matthew. Poor in spirit—i.e., one who in
humility trusts only in God? Hardly! They'd be more like
the Pharisee mentioned in one of Jesus' parables who
prayed to himself, "I thank you I'm not like everyone
else." How about mourning over sins? No—not their
own sins, anyway. Meekness so that their spirits were
under control? Uh-uh. They used their position and influence as leverage to dominate and intimidate. Then what
about hungering and thirsting for righteousness? Well,
perhaps—if you mean an external right-ness that others
notice. But certainly not the kind that comes from a
heart that is aflamed by the Spirit of God. And don't
even ask about mercy, purity of heart, peacemaking,
and persecution for righteousness' sake.

Apples and Apple Trees
Jesus isn't overly impressed with churchy activity.
The Sermon on the Mount isn't just about doing more.
It isn't just trying to get people to tithe, attend church
more often, or evangelize more robustly.

It's so easy for religion to be dumbed down into little

more than religious activity. Churches are filled with people who know how to go through the motions. They sing, they pray, they give, they study. But what's on the inside? What are they becoming?

Why do Christians continue to bring consumer appetites to church, constantly asking how their needs can be met? Why doesn't it bother them that the gap is widening between the wealthy and the poor of the world? Why do they support political policies that favor themselves rather than the powerless of the world? Why do they pass on scandalous rumors, devour one another with angry words, and fail to keep commitments?

Could it be that we've reduced Christ-following to a lowest common denominator of socially-acceptable church attendance? Could it be that we've found it easier to do a bunch of religious stuff without worrying about the much harder task of daily transformation into the image of Christ?

Second and third generation Christians especially face the temptation to inherit faith without ever really owning it. Many hang on to Christian traditions, Christian language, and Christian doctrine without the inner commitment of earlier disciples. Religion then becomes a sedative, a simple narcotic that keeps us from having to confront the deeper chambers of our lives.

Jesus wants us to say, "More than anything else I long to be God's. I want to become like him. I want him to change me inside out." If that isn't your commitment, your righteousness may be like the freezer that was left unplugged: shiny on the outside, but putrid on the inside.

Again, Dallas Willard gets to the heart of the matter:

One must aim to become the kind of person from whom the deeds of the law naturally flow. The apple

36

tree naturally and easily produces apples because of its
inner nature. This is the most crucial thing to remember
if we would understand Jesus' picture of the kingdom
heart given in the Sermon on the Mount.[4]

Two Questions

A couple questions to close this chapter. The first
one I ask very quietly, maybe in just a whisper. How
much like the religious leaders are we? If we guard our
positions of honor and consume our time over minutia,
how close are we? If we major in the letter of the law
and not in the spirit of the law, how close are we? If
church members are deep in religious snobbery and
very shallow in that inner zeal for God—well, we need
to listen carefully to the words of Jesus.

It's always easier, of course, to see it in another
person. I can't help but think of "Linda." Year after year,
I watched her sour attitudes and her bitterness devour
everyone around her. I saw her shaking her head in
disapproval nearly every time I preached. I kept meeting
people she had gutted with her words. But people
always protected her. "That's just how she is. You know,
she does some wonderful things." It's like no one
expected anything more. That's how she is. Yes, she
keeps harming people. But she does good things.

Why have we settled for such meager attempts at
discipleship? Why don't we expect people, over a period
of time, to start to exhibit Christian characteristics like
love, joy, peace, and kindness?

The second question is for your personal reflection:
As a person on your own spiritual pilgrimage, where are
you going? I'm not wondering if you're doing more
things. Rather, are you honestly seeking to become
someone in Christ's image?

If you aren't, something must change! You must yield your life to God, because he isn't looking for the righteousness of the scribes and Pharisees. That's a broad road that many travel, but a road that leads to destruction (Matt. 7:13-14).

Two men went to the church to pray. One kept all the rules, was known as a generous giver to good causes, and thought he knew just where he stood with God. He was thankful he wasn't like most of the other people he knew. He bowed from his pew and uttered this pray, "Dear Lord, I thank you that I'm not like these other people." The other man came into the church building, fell down at the communion table, and choked out his prayer: "Dear Lord, have mercy on me a sinner. Here I am again—deeply in need of your grace. Break me. Melt me. Mold me. Fill me."

With which of these do you suppose the Lord was pleased?

Chapter 3
MURDER WAITING TO HATCH

Anger and contempt are the twin scourges of the earth.
Mingled with greed and sexual lust . . . these bitter
emotions form the poisonous brew in which human
existence stands suspended. Few people ever get free of
them in this life, and for most of us even old age does
not bring relief.[1]

Alice came into my office looking as if she'd been wrestling a cougar. Her color was drained; her hair was disheveled; her eyes were lava. Friends had already tipped me off with a simple diagnosis: depression. Doesn't every minister have a "five easy steps out of depression" pep talk, they must have wondered.

But quite often depression is only the exterior layer. Lurking behind the ghost of depression is often the goblin of anger—bitter, unresolved anger.

Quickly Alice's story unfolded. Her whole life she had felt like Cinderella without the fairy godmother, the royal ball, or the glass slipper. Her sisters were more attractive and more intelligent. They were the objects of her parents' attention. Even though her mom and dad would say the words "I love you" to her, she never really believed it.

One memory haunted her, nearly possessed her. She recalled a Christmas she had asked for a $50 gift and was told they just didn't have the money. After her initial disappointment, Alice accepted that. But when she walked into the living room on Christmas morning, a heat seeking missile hit her. Her sisters had brand new bikes, each worth over $100.

Now Alice's life was unraveling quickly. She couldn't relate well to those who tried to befriend her. Her grades were well below her ability. Her spiritual life was perfunctory. And, perhaps worst of all, she wondered if her plight in life was God's judgment on her.

Unless she could allow God to deal with her hatred, she was facing a gloomy, depressing life.

The Tracks of Anger

Many of the tracks of anger are apparent: they're reported each morning in the newspaper. And we wonder: Why are the violent crimes of murder, assault, and rape so common around us? Why so much spousal and child abuse? Why so many hate crimes?

But anger's tracks are found everywhere—not just in the headlines. We're just used to them. We've grown accustomed to road rage, airport rage ("We're delayed *how* long?" "My bags accidentally went to *where*?"), and e-mail rage.

The impact of anger is apparent in the broken or bruised relationships all around. In my own community, I've heard too many stories of alienation that go back many, many years—some don't even know the exact starting point—to feelings of anger.

There is school rage, roommate rage, marriage rage, workplace rage, neighborhood rage, political rage, radio rage, and, yes, even church rage.

I have a wonderful vantage point to witness unbridled rage. And I don't mean as a minister. I am a little league coach for baseball and basketball. Talk about anger! Just last week I witnessed a grown man (on the other bench) stomping around, throwing his jacket on the ground, complaining about how the refs—teenage boys making minimum wage—were cheating his team. He was basketball's Oliver Stone—complete with irrational conspiracy theories. (I think he was just upset that he was being outcoached!) Eventually, he picked up his jacket and marched out of the gym saying he couldn't take it any more.

Can you say, "IT'S JUST A GAME"?

We're an angry society, and the anger is taking its toll! We get worn out either by lashing out in rage—almost addicted to the high octane fuel of hurt feelings and hatred—or by depression, which is often an attempt to restrain or deny anger.

Too many are like the woman who was bitten by a dog and was suspected of having rabies. She went to the hospital and was ready to have tests done when an eager intern began talking to her, perhaps telling her too much. He described all the terrible things that could happen to someone with rabies. Before he knew it, all the blood had drained out of her face. Then he left for a while, and when he returned she was writing some things down. Occasionally she'd look up and think, then look down and write again.

He thought, "Oh, no. I've scared her into writing a will. She thinks she's going to die." So he interrupted her: "I hope I didn't scare you into thinking you're going to die tomorrow. Is that a will you're writing?"

She looked up and replied, "No, it's not a will. In

case I'm infected, I'm making a list of all the people I want to bite before I die!"

That would be the way to go, wouldn't it? Go out in a blaze of retaliation! That's what hostility does to us.

Is Anger Sinful?

I think it's significant that Jesus' first illustration of what a kingdom-ready heart looks like deals with the removal of anger.

> You have heard that it was said to the people long ago, "Do not murder, and anyone who murders will be subject to judgment." But I tell you that anyone who is angry with a brother or sister will be subject to judgment.
>
> Matt. 5:21-22

But is anger always a sin? Before answering, you might recall a couple of scenes from Jesus' life.

In Mark 3 Jesus sees the hypocritical spirit of the Pharisees. These influential religious leaders were more concerned about the details of their traditions than they were about the plight of a man with a withered hand. Mark tells us that Jesus "looked around at them in anger," being "deeply distressed at their stubborn hearts."

We can try to soften it a bit and call this "righteous indignation," but that may be too fine a point for Mark. He just says Jesus was angry—and for a good reason.

The word *anger* doesn't pop up in John 2, but Jesus is again clearly upset. Jesus found people setting up currency exchanges in the temple courts. As foreign Jews would come in with their money, they'd need to purchase an animal for sacrifice. But the money changers had made a mockery of the temple setting. So Jesus made a whip and went to work. He drove them out, exclaiming: "Get these out of here! Stop turning my Father's house into a market!"

If we believe that Jesus never sinned, then we have to conclude that anger isn't always wrong. But, honestly, this is dangerous for us. Because it has often become a way for people to excuse their destructive feelings and behavior. Self-deception allows them to believe that they, too, experience only "righteous indignation." Sure, they often simmer and sometimes explode—at coworkers, at politicians, at spouses, and at children. But they're just doing—so they tell themselves!—what Jesus did when he saw misbehavior.

Perhaps it helps to understand that anger is, initially, a feeling that arises spontaneously. It's a response to a stimulus that comes through one or more of our senses. Before your conscious mind ever kicks in gear, you're angry.

You're awakened at 2:00 a.m. by a noise in the kitchen and suddenly your body starts pumping adrenalin. Or someone cuts you off in traffic, making you think your life is in danger. Anger is there. Now . . . what are you going to do with it?

Choice Kicks In

You're not directly responsible for these spontaneous feelings of anger. But you are responsible for what you choose to do with them. Will you indulge them? Or will you move beyond them?

Jesus, in illustrating the right heart, isn't talking about that emotional response. He's concerned with the next stage, when the mind takes over and makes a choice. Will you choose bitterness and resentment? Or will you, out of love for your brother or sister, reconcile? Will you quit treating your spouse or children with anger—maybe simmering with icy anger or exploding in molten anger—or will you choose to continue those old patterns? Will you live in love or rage? That's the choice Jesus is pressing.

> *Again, anyone who says to a brother or sister, "Raca," is answerable to the Sanhedrin. And anyone who says, "You fool!" will be in danger of the fire of hell.*

Aren't you glad he warned us not to uses the word "raca"? You've probably never really been tempted to turn to your boss and yell, "Raca," have you? I haven't, and I'm always glad to find things like that in the Bible that I won't ever break.

It isn't that simple, of course. "Raca" is an Aramaic term of contempt. It might correspond to any number of contemptuous words we're familiar with. "Idiot!" "Moron!" "Loser!" "Nitwit!" "Geek!" Anger has a way of growing quickly into contempt.

You've surely noticed before, haven't you, how arguments often wind up a long place from where they begin? An argument that begins as a discussion over someone's propensity for being late soon turns into a nuclear war focusing on in-laws, weight, or intelligence. That's what Jesus speaks about here.

But he knows that in this war, bigger and bigger weapons of mass destruction get pulled out of the arsenal. So he warns about calling someone a fool. Based on what "fool" means in the Old Testament, he's probably referring to someone being a moral fool.[2] We're not just attacking personality now; we're zeroing in on their moral character. That's the best way to injure someone, isn't it? Just drop some hints here and there that they're not the person they seem to be. This is malice at its seamiest.

Here's the progression, then. Anger strikes—evolving into bitterness and resentment. Then this hatred turns vicious and degrading.

This, according to our Teacher, is the spirit of murder. It's murder in the embryo stage. The Pharisees could read the sixth commandment and forbid murder. No guns. No knives. No killing. But Jesus is pointing us to the heart of God represented in that command-ment. It isn't just that God disallows murder; rather, God seeks hearts of love. "Love your neighbor as your-self," Jesus would say is the second great command (Matt. 22:34-40).

Most of us are safe with the reductionistic reading of the Pharisees. But if we hear the challenge of Jesus, we have much deeper searching to do. We have to think of all the collateral damage around us from our poisonous thoughts and venomous words.

A woman once told the famous evangelist Billy Sunday, "There's nothing wrong with losing my temper. I blow up and then it's all over." Sunday responded, "So does a shotgun. Look at the damage it leaves behind."

Three Ways to Handle Anger

There are at least three ways to try to manage the anger in our lives. One is to vent it. Just let it all fly out. One teenager who took this approach was angry at being cut from his high school basketball team in the Los Angeles area. So he went home, grabbed a baseball bat, and smashed windows, lamps, appliances, and other household items. His mother ran to a neighbor's house for safety. Then he took his father's rifle and being firing around the house. By the time he was finished, he had done $20,000 in damage.

Maybe venting can be the lesser of evils. Better to

beat your pillow than your boss, don't you think? But the choice to vent can also condition your body to welcome the rush. "Let's do this some more!" And it doesn't get at the real problem.

So often, when we vent our anger, it's in the form of a personal attack that we'll later regret. As an old hymn I sang growing up warned:

> Angry words are lightly spoken,
> Bitterest thoughts are rashly stirred,
> Brightest links of life are broken—
> By a single angry word.

A former member of my church blew up in anger one week. In a moment of rage, he whipped off a letter demanding that I be fired—a letter he immediately mailed to all the church leaders. Later he admitted sheepishly that he didn't believe everything he'd said, and that he should have slept on the letter before mailing it out—or at least should have spoken *to* me rather than *about* me first.

Vent-ers always run the risk of sabotaging their own lives. Because the ones they vent against tend to be the ones closest to them. They rarely vent with Saddam Hussein. They vent, rather, with a spouse, a child, a parent, or a coworker.

A second possibility is to suppress our anger. Just squash it down, send it underground, sweep it under the rug, pretend it's not there.

Tick . . . tick . . . tick . . . tick. (Can you hear the bomb about to explode?)

A lot of marriages are slowly destroyed by suppressed anger. A spouse gets mad, but wants to be a good Christian person. So she sweeps the irritation under the rug. When confronted by her husband she says, courageously, "No, I'm not angry with you. A little disappointed, yes, but not angry." She thinks she's doing the right thing, but watch out!

The neighbors may say, "That's such a lovely couple. They never have a cross word." But just because they never fight doesn't mean the marriage is a joy-filled relationship. They may have forfeited warmth and tenderness along the way by pretending that anger wasn't a barrier. Chances are good that they'll wind up like a 3-liter container of Coke that's sat for a month without the cap. There is no fizz.

We've got to have some positive way to resolve anger and conflict, because it will be there. And trust me—I've seen this again and again as a minister—it will come out one way or another. Those deep feelings will be on slow burn, and they may seep out through withholding sex or by complimenting other men or women (as a way of comparing your spouse unfavorably). It may come out as silence, as depression, as acting hurt, or as an affair.

This leaves us with a third choice, then. Venting solves nothing. Suppressing only makes matters linger.

The third option is difficult. Frankly, my personality type tends to run from it. It is the difficult job of reconciling.

Yet this is a wonderful possibility. You don't have to be blown around by the fierce winds of your anger. You can refuse the illusion of "external control psychology," which says that you are at the mercy of what's happened to you. For example, a husband might say, "She made me mad." No, she didn't. She may have done something irritating. But you chose at some point to be mad. You chose whether to hold onto the anger or to work through it.

You can choose to punish, criticize, nag, withdraw, or badger. Or, with a heart shaped by the kingdom of God, you can choose to accept, forgive, resolve, support, and love.

Here is what Jesus says to do:

Therefore, if you are offering your gift at the altar and there remember that the brother or sister has something against you, leave your gift there in front of the altar. First go and be reconciled to that person; then come and offer your gift.
Matt. 5:23-24

It's a sacred moment. You're at the temple, ready to offer your gift to God. But at the last moment, you think about a relationship that's been damaged. You remember the brokenness, the anger, the bitterness. So you hit the pause button at worship and you leave to seek reconciliation.

Notice: you initiate it. Maybe you've caused most of the damage (Matt. 5:23-24); maybe the other person did (Matt. 18:15-20). But either way, you seek reconciliation. You don't want to be a person of malice and bitterness. You have learned that the rule of God is changing us into people who live with love.

Jesus said to *go directly to that person*. There's one huge hurdle, of course. Pride. Pride wants us to receive reconciliation and apologies not initiate them. "If he wants to solve this with me, he can come like a snake on his belly!"

Here's how it might work in marriage. "You mentioned to me that I'm spending too much time away from the family. Everything in me wants to fight about that—because I need time to have fun. But I want to talk through this. Because it's more important for us to be right than for me to be right."

Or it could sound like this: "You know it really rattles my cage when you talk on the phone all evening to your mother when we have hardly spoken. But I don't want to be bitter about this. Can we talk about it and find something we can both live with?"

In addition to telling us to go directly to the person for "conflict resolution," Jesus also said to *go quickly*. Don't keep fooling yourself that someday you'll get around to it. As the Apostle Paul said, "Do not let the sun go down while you are still angry, and do not give the devil a foothold" (Eph. 4:26f).

Every golfer knows that a divot needs to be fixed immediately. If you replace the turf immediately, it will be fine. But you can't return a week later to try to fix it. The grass it dead by then.

The same with relationships. Don't wait for attitudes to harden and spirits to wither. While anger can be molded, while it's fresh, process it with the person with whom you're angry.

The Journey Begins With a Step

After contemplating the words of Jesus, it's very likely that you might need to exhume some skeletons of bitterness toward a parent, a child, a spouse—maybe an employer or employee.

Whatever the relationship, and however old the skeleton may be, don't let the sun go down on your anger again. The journey of reconciliation and renewed love begins with one step.

Just this morning I received a note from a former member of our church who had listened on cassette tape to a message I'd given. He wrote (and I include this with his permission):

As a result of your sermon, I spoke to my brother again for the first time in two years. I tried to make amends to him two years ago and it went badly. I left it up to him to "get back to me." I called him again and things went better. I don't think he will ever call me on his own or take an active interest in our lives but it won't be because of my pride. Thank you.

That's just the kind of step I'm talking about. It may feel like a baby step, but according to Jesus it's a huge leap. Will you take it?

Chapter 4
SAFE SEX

You have heard that it was said, "Do not commit adultery."
But I tell you that anyone who looks at a woman lustfully
has already committed adultery with her in her heart.
—Matthew 5:27f

Bilbo Baggins had just retrieved a two-handled cup and taken it back to the dwarves. It was a moment of profound joy! For this cup had been plucked from the treasure-trove that had been stolen from the dwarves years ago. They had enlisted the help of this hobbit, Bilbo Baggins, hoping that some of his mother's adventuresome genes might emerge. Now, finally at the mountain where their stolen treasures had been taken, they celebrated this first recovered item. But the celebration changed quickly because of the fierce dragon, Smaug, who was guarding all the loot. Tolkien says:

> *The dwarves were still passing the cup from hand to*
> *hand and talking delightedly of the recovery of their trea-*
> *sure, when suddenly a vast rumbling woke in the moun-*
> *tain underneath as if it was an old volcano that had*
> *made up its mind to start eruptions once again. The door*
> *behind them was pulled nearly to, and blocked from*

51

closing with a stone, but up the long tunnel came the dreadful echoes, from far down in the depths, of a bellowing and a trampling that made the ground beneath them tremble.

Then the dwarves forgot their joy and their confident boasts of a moment before and cowered down in fright. Smaug was still to be reckoned with. It does not do to leave a live dragon out of your calculations, if you live near him.[1]

That's a bit of good advice, isn't it? Never leave a dragon out of your calculations, if you live near him. Those seem like good words to remember in this chapter as we investigate Jesus' words about sexuality.

You Can't Hide

Where would you go today to try to escape all the highly sexual images that surround you? Can you think of a place?

Well, the grocery store is out. The magazines at the checkout stand are full of glossy pictures begging you to purchase them. Next to the pictures are titillating headlines, promising to tell you more about sexual fulfillment or about the sex lives of stars: "What Really Happened to _____?" You can fill in the blank from week to week—Britney, J-Lo, Tom, Hugh, Madonna. The names change but the stories look familiar.

You know better than to suggest the movie theater— or even your favorite recliner in front of the television, for that matter. Despite all the protests about sexuality and violence in movies, the writers and producers know what sells.

And the internet? A ten billion dollar per year pornography industry has found the perfect environment for their sales. The privacy of these chat rooms, newsgroups, and web sites has made the internet a "safe" place for sexual fantasies to be stoked. The fact that hours are drained, marriages are damaged, children are ignored, and hearts are hardened by cybersex hardly matters to these purveyors of porn.

There really isn't a place where you can escape, is there? I joined several friends a few years ago to climb Mt. Kilimanjaro. What could be further from temptation than joining a bunch of other guys on a mountain in Tanzania?

But the first morning, after we'd hiked hard in a driving rain the night before, I rose early, tired of trying to sleep. I walked outside the hut at 5:00 a.m., and not far away in the mist was a beautiful woman in a tiny teal t-shirt and tight jeans (as I faintly recall!) leaning over to brush her hair. Turns out this was a British supermodel named, of course, Nikki. She was hiking with a television crew from ABC to film a special program. They were on the same hiking schedule as our group, so for six days we hiked up and down Mt. Kilimanjaro with Nikki.

You Can Run. But You Can't Hide!

Even if there were no "Nikki," any place you go you carry the hard drive of your mind's storage capacity with all the images, all the commercials, and all the photos downloaded.

Jesus' words couldn't be more contemporary. As he speaks to the need for sexual purity in our behavior and in our thoughts, his words ring fresh in this sex-saturated world.

Sex Is God's Idea

Let's make sure we understand this: sex itself isn't the problem. There's nothing bad or dirty about sex. Some of the leaders of the early church—like Origen who said that sex is evil, or Augustine who wrote that sex is a result of the Fall (Genesis 3)—were wrong.

God himself is the author of sexuality. He made us male and female. He's the one who came up with the idea. In my Bible classes at Abilene Christian University—filled with students who are eighteen and nineteen—I try to emphasize this. There is so much degradation of sexuality around them and they've heard so many warnings about sexual immorality, that it's easy for them to forget that God is behind our sexual impulses.

Someone has said that in the beginning God created a companion for Adam so he wouldn't be lonely. And he made the companion a female so they wouldn't be bored! God instructed them to become "one flesh," which obviously refers in part to their sexual relationship (and the intimacy supporting it).

I've found that one way to get even the most reluctant university student to enjoy Bible class is to introduce them to the Song of Solomon, the Bible's PG-13 book. This small slice of scripture celebrates the longing of a husband and wife for one another. Pay attention as he looks at his beloved and describes her:

> *How beautiful your sandaled feet,*
> *O prince's daughter!*
> *Your graceful legs are like jewels,*
> *the work of a craftsman's hands.*
> *Your navel is a rounded goblet*
> *that never lacks blended wine.*
> *Your waist is a mound of wheat*
> *encircled by lilies.*
> *Your breasts are like two fawns,*
> *twins of a gazelle.*
> *Your neck is like an ivory tower.*

Your eyes are the pools of Heshbon
by the gate of Bath Rabbim.
Your nose is like the tower of Lebanon
looking toward Damascus.
Your head crowns you like Mount Carmel.
Your hair is like royal tapestry;
the king is held captive by its tresses.
How beautiful you are and how pleasing,
O love, with your delights!
Your stature is like that of the palm,
and your breasts like clusters of fruit.
I said, "I will climb the palm tree;
I will take hold of its fruit."

Song of Solomon 7:1-8

Would you call that a frank discussion of sexual delight? It's a bit hard to miss the point. He's thankful for the gift of sex!

God loves us enough to give this enjoyable gift. But he also loves us enough to tell us how the gift may be used without damaging our lives.

The consistent witness of scripture and of the church is that God demands chastity: sexual abstinence in singleness and fidelity in marriage (the covenanted union of a man and a woman).

This is, of course, quite different from cultural norms. The perspective that any sexual relationship is all right as long as it involves two consenting adults is foreign to the biblical story. Richard Hays is frank about our culture's misled blindness concerning sexual gratification:

Despite the smooth illusions perpetrated by mass culture
in the United States, sexual gratification is not a sacred
right, and celibacy is not a fate worse than death. . . .
While mandatory priestly celibacy is unbiblical, a life of

sexual abstinence can promote "good order and unhindered devotion to the Lord" (1 Cor. 7:35). Surely it is a matter of some interest for Christian ethics that both Jesus and Paul lived without sexual relationships.[2]

To describe sex outside of marriage, the Bible uses words like "adultery" and "fornication"—the former meaning sexual relations by someone who is married with someone other than their spouse and the latter being a broader word meaning immorality, whether it's premarital or extramarital.

The limitation is clear in scripture: no sex outside of marriage. That may seem narrow and prehistoric to some, but that doesn't change God's plan. He made us, and he knows how to protect us. He knows that "safe sex" is ultimately not about wearing a condom. As the one who wired us, he recognizes that there are more fears than just sexually transmitted diseases. There is also sexually transmitted distrust, sexually transmitted disappointment, and sexually transmitted anxiety.

For a sexual relationship to be truly safe and life-affirming, there has to be a committed relationship—a marriage. Only with someone whom you have covenanted with for life are you free to enjoy this gift of God without fear.

The church's teaching about sexual purity must be anchored in this belief that the God of creation is a good, wise, redeeming God who seeks to bless us. Our central reason for avoiding immorality has little to do with sexually transmitted diseases or with unplanned pregnancies (though we've seen the devastating consequences). Rather, we focus on our allegiance to God and his word. We instruct our teenagers and our college students—as well as everyone else!—that the reign of God has broken in, calling for obedient hearts.

Serious Christ-followers hear his admonitions about purity and seek to follow him.

Later the Apostle Paul would put the whole discussion in a Christ-centered perspective:

> *The body . . . is not meant for sexual immorality but for the Lord, and the Lord for the body. By his power God raised the Lord from the dead, and he will raise us also. Do you not know that your bodies are members of Christ himself? . . . Flee from sexual immorality. All other sins people commit are outside their bodies, but those who sin sexually sin against their own bodies. Do you not know that your bodies are temples of the Holy Spirit, who is in you, whom you have received from God? You are not your own; you were bought at a price. Therefore honor God with your bodies.*

1 Cor. 6:13-15, 18-20

The Seventh Commandment

Both Jesus and the Pharisees recognized that adultery, as explicitly spelled out in the seventh commandment, is wrong. Marriage means a commitment to be faithful to one's spouse, resisting whatever temptations may arise.

As a minister, I've heard the heart-wrenching stories of families who have suffered because a wife or husband chose not to honor their vows. I've seen jobs lost, relationships destroyed, children devastated, and reputations ruined. No wonder God said it clearly: you shall NOT commit adultery.

But there is more to that seventh commandment than the Pharisees taught, Jesus says. Once again, their interest was limited to the external, minimal requirements. But, as Jesus instructs us, sex is much more than just pulling the sheets back on a bed. It involves your mind and heart. You can break the seventh commandment without ever touching another person!

He offers the broader principle later: "Out of the heart come evil thoughts, murder, adultery, sexual immorality, theft, false testimony, slander" (Matt. 15:19). It's the heart that Jesus is ultimately concerned with. The reign of God among us means that we eliminate not just sexual immorality but also the lust behind the actions.

Let me offer a word of clarification about what Jesus is *not* saying. When he warns us not to look lustfully, he certainly wasn't saying that looking at someone and finding them attractive is a sin. Nor was he saying that looking and having a sexual thought is wrong. Christians have experienced far too much false guilt by thinking that Jesus is forbidding every sexual thought.

Remember this: God is the one who made us male and female. He wired us as sexual beings, capable of finding others attractive and of having sexual thoughts about them.

Let me take this even one step further: sexual temptation that comes from sexual thoughts and feelings isn't wrong. Jesus, who was tempted in all ways even as we are (according the writer of Hebrews), was without sin (Heb. 4:15). It isn't the temptation that is wrong; it's caving in to the temptation.

There's a helpful parallel with the first illustration about anger. Anger itself isn't always wrong. But there is a point where our human choice enters and we allow the anger to become contempt, hatred, and bitterness. We face a decision: Will we release the anger, having processed it, or will we welcome it and permit it to devolve into something worse?

The same is true of sexual thoughts. A thought pops

in—you find someone attractive, you have a sexual thought, you're even tempted. But now—what will you do with this thought? Will you allow it to remain and turn it into a fantasy? Or will you release it and move on?

A good translation of Matthew 5:28 is essential. The words of Jesus as reported by Matthew focus on intention: "Whoever looks at a woman *for the purpose of lusting* after her . . . ." This is a salacious gaze, a lecherous stare. This is looking at someone to disrobe them, looking in order to lust, looking as if they were an object for your desire.

There are some clear differences between natural desires and lust. For one thing, desire appreciates the beauty of another person, while lust uses the other person as an object for selfish purposes. Appropriate desire feels a natural attraction; lust becomes obsessed with seducing another person while maybe even knowing you could never get away with it. Lust sometimes even thoughtfully and secretly makes plans to fulfill the desires, even if it's against God's will.

Charlie Shedd shared with his son before his marriage some words his wife had given him: "God doesn't keep the birds of temptation from flying over our heads. He only asks that we keep them from building nests in our hair!"

Eye Poking

If Jesus doesn't already have your attention, he certainly does when he talks about the extent to which you should go to preserve pure thoughts:

> If your right eye causes you to stumble, gouge it out and throw it away. It is better for you to lose one part of your body than for your whole body to be thrown into hell. And if your right hand causes you to stumble, cut it off

> *and throw it away. It is better for you to lose one part of*
> *your body than for your whole body to go into hell.*
> Matt. 5:29-30

Unfortunately, some, like Origen who castrated himself, have taken these words literally. But Jesus was using hyperbole, pointing us to the urgency of the matter. Since lust is embedded in your heart, poking out your eyes or whacking off a hand wouldn't necessarily even get to the real problem!

But recognizing this as hyperbole doesn't diminish the urgent call. If you're looking at something you shouldn't, quit looking! If your feet are taking you to places that cause your mind to wander where it shouldn't, don't go there! If your hands are holding materials that fill your mind with sexual fantasies, empty them! If your computer is downloading images to your mind, turn it off! By all means, stop feeding the lusts.

Why play with pornography? Why read certain romantic novels that escort you into a frustrating land of unfulfilled fantasies? I have no desire to lay down specific rules about what books you can and can't read and what movies you can and can't watch. Levels of self-control and vulnerability to temptation vary considerably. But you know you, and you know your weaknesses. Feeding your lusts is like trying to extinguish a forest fire by dropping lighter fluid from a plane.

But that's not to say this is just a personal battle. Those I've known who have successfully fought this battle against lust are people who recognized that Jesus' words were to a new community.

Every Christ-follower needs a small community of friends and mentors with whom they can be completely honest. Nothing disarms temptation quite like exposure:

telling someone whom you trust, someone who cares deeply about you, that you struggle.

This is an area where the works of Ecclesiastes are definitely true: "Two are better than one. . . . If one falls down, his friend can help him up" (Eccles. 4:9f).

Even as I write these words, there are faces in mind of Christian brothers who have walked this journey with me. We have openly confessed our struggles with one another. We know the desires of our hearts—that we want to be faithful to our wives and even more that we want to be faithful to God—and yet we know the temptations before us. We have confessed, prayed, encouraged, and challenged.

We've reminded each other of this: God doesn't reject people who struggle. God's words of rejection are preserved for people who cease struggling and march away from him in obstinance.

Lust is not the unpardonable sin. It isn't the one thing that can spiritually defeat you. But the kingdom of God has broken in! Through his power, you can continue allowing him to change you inside out.

Chapter 5
LIFETIME LOVE

It has been said, "Anyone who divorces his wife must give her a certificate of divorce." But I tell you that anyone who divorces his wife, except for sexual immorality, causes her to become an adulteress, and anyone who marries the divorced woman commits adultery.
—Matthew 5:31f

As I write this chapter a few weeks before our twenty-fifth wedding anniversary, a smile keeps creeping across my face. I'm remembering the bold, naive promises we made to each other: "for better, for worse; for richer, for poorer; in sickness, in health; until death do us part."

You'd think someone older would warn you, "Run like the wind! You have no idea what you're saying!" But the oldest person in the wedding ceremony was the preacher. He was all of twenty-two. In other words, no one knew any better than to let us make such broad, sweeping promises.

Thankfully. Because now we look back and realize that those promises, reflecting our pledge to follow Jesus in this upside down kingdom, have sustained us when we were too tired to work on the marriage.

There was just no way to see what was coming. We couldn't have predicted the unbelievable joy of welcoming three babies into this world. Nor could we have imagined the heartbreak of learning our daughter was mentally handicapped, of watching her later morph from a vibrant, healthy child into a feeble, ailing one, and of standing over her as she took the last few breaths of her life at the age of ten.

There was no way to know we would go month after month, even year after year with very little sleep. For much of her life, Megan only slept a couple of hours a night. It was as if she knew she didn't have long on this earth and she wasn't going to waste any time in bed! But it wore us out.

Nor could we have predicted the dark journey of grief—a journey where it was, for a couple of years, hard to find each other.

And yet today I couldn't be more thankful that those vows have stuck. I'm so thankful that during one of those dark spells we didn't throw in the towel. For through the mountains and valleys we have learned what it means for two to be made one by God. I just looked back in my journal from a year ago. I was in a beautiful part of Africa, preparing to speak at a missions conference. Surrounded by Lake Victoria, surging trees, a blue sky, full-bloomed flowers, and dozens of species of birds, I wrote:

> *The moment is nearly perfect, as I prepare for the East Africa Men's Retreat. But not quite perfect. For I'm nine time zones away from Diane. Humor is only half funny if she isn't there to laugh. Beauty is a bit unformed if she isn't around to enjoy it. Her blue eyes are the prism through which all beauty comes fully alive.*

All right. I'm not a poet. But this isn't so much poetry as prose: an account of life together as love has matured and deepened.

Marriage is difficult. We ought to tell every young couple that during their premarital counseling.

Some of our best friends in the world have been featured for many years on the cover of an album filled with music for weddings. It is the perfect wedding: a true Hallmark moment as they stand at the altar with their large wedding party.

But that one picture doesn't tell *the rest of the story*. It doesn't show their car slipping off a bridge just outside town a few moments later as they were chased by friends. (Think what it would be like had they been enemies!) It doesn't show them checking into the ER just hours after the wedding ceremony as a result of the wreck. Nor does it picture them checking into their honeymoon suite at 4:00 a.m. with scratches and bruises all over.

We spend so much time getting ready for wedding ceremonies, don't we? Even then, they never go perfectly. The bride is nervous. The groom is scared out of his wits, trying to decide how big to smile: too little looks like he regrets the decision and too much looks like his mind is on later events!

But it's the marriage, not the ceremony, that really takes the work.

Divorce's Impact

It's no wonder that Jesus' third illustration of fulfilling God's true intentions centers on marriage. For he knows (as he mentions in Matthew 19) that God is the one who joins a couple together. He binds them together and intends for no one to rip them apart.

And that's just what it is: a ripping. I used to be reticent about preaching on divorce, knowing there are so many in church who have been through the pain. But I've found that they are the very ones insisting that the church be honest enough to tell people what it's like. That isn't to say that, regretfully, it hasn't been necessary at times; but even then it's a sign of brokenness.

The truth is that divorce is extracting a terrible price on people all around us. I've heard some Christian leaders rail against homosexuality as the #1 enemy of the traditional family. They're wrong. Divorce is the #1 enemy of the traditional family. It's just harder to say that when many of your viewers, listeners, and congregants have been divorced.

This culture shows few signs of changing course. We are surrounded by a therapeutic worldview where the goal is for each individual to be happy and fulfilled. The church has too often followed that lead. Richard Hays is right on target:

> The collapse of cultural strictures against divorce has left the church in serious need of fresh theological and pastoral reflection about divorce and remarriage. The pain and complications of divorce cast their shadows across almost every congregation, yet the church often fails to address the issue forthrightly. In some churches divorce remains a taboo, and divorced persons are ostracized. In other churches, however, divorce is treated almost casually, and members are not in any serious way held accountable to their marriage vows. . .
>
> Insofar as there has been any theological rationale at all for this historic shift, it lies in the conviction that we must avoid being judgmental . . . . If someone opts out of a marriage commitment, that is his or her own business, and no one else should presume to pass judgment. Furthermore, if the gospel is a word of grace, so the

thinking goes, then we must at all costs avoid legalism. To require people to stay in difficult marriages against their inclination would be to impose a harsh law contrary to the spirit of love. I am persuaded that this line of thought has had disastrous consequences for the church.[1]

These challenging words of discipleship from Jesus in Matthew 5 return us to God's intentions for marriage as the union of a man and woman. Jesus doesn't describe divorce as some irredeemable form of sin and evil; rather, he points us to the way of God's love.

Moses and Marriage

The instruction Jesus quoted ("It has been said . . . .") was from the teaching of Moses in Deuteronomy 24. The Pharisees obviously were interpreting this text in a different way than Jesus.

Moses was addressing a situation that had arisen in Israel. In this fallen world—so far from God's original intentions—people were divorcing. So under God's guidance he instructed them what to do:

If a man marries a woman who becomes displeasing to him because he finds something indecent about her, and he writes her a certificate of divorce, gives it to her and sends her from his house, and if after she leaves his house she becomes the wife of another man, and her second husband dislikes her and writes her a certificate of divorce, gives it to her and sends her from his house, or if he dies, then her first husband, who divorced her, is not allowed to marry her again after she has been defiled. That would be detestable in the eyes of the Lord. Do not bring sin upon the land the Lord your God is giving you as an inheritance.

Deut. 24:1-4

Once again the Pharisees and teachers of the law had skirted God's deeper intentions by focusing on the mere letter of the law. They found in this Deuteronomy text an endorsement and even advocacy for divorce. Two things from that text especially intrigued them.

One is the certificate of divorce. That seemed like an obvious permission slip from God. A man could hand it to his wife, and he was free. (They couldn't imagine in their world the reverse situation.)

The other is the reference to the "unclean thing." In the time of Jesus, there was a controversy that was fresh on the minds of the people. Apparently most people lined up behind the interpretations of two popular rabbis, Shammai and Hillel. Shammai was more restrictive, claiming that "unclean thing" refers to adultery. Hillel cast a very broad interpretation, claiming that there are many things that fit this category. Perhaps a man's wife is unable to bear children or speaks disrespectfully to his parents or burns his food or is quarrelsome. Whatever it may be, if it was displeasing to her husband, he could divorce her.

In Matthew 19 these two things are in the foreground when the Pharisees quiz Jesus about marriage and divorce: "Some Pharisees came to him to test him. They asked, 'Is it lawful to a man to divorce his wife for any and every reason?'" (Matt. 19:3).

Notice that they came to him to test him. They weren't sincerely searching for truth. They weren't eager to find out how the message of God's kingdom might place claims upon their lives. They just wanted to catch him contradicting the law of Moses and to pull him into the current controversies about how to interpret that law. What are the reasons? What is the unclean thing? What about the certificate of divorce?

The marriage-wrecking approach of these loophole lawyers missed the whole spirit of scripture. Jesus said that to understand God's will, you can't begin in Deuteronomy 24—a text that seeks to limit harm in a fallen world. To find his true intentions you must return to the very beginning.

> *So the Lord God caused the man to fall into a deep sleep; and while he was sleeping, he took one of the man's ribs and closed up the place with flesh. Then the Lord God made a woman from the rib he had taken out of the man, and he brought her to the man. The man said, "This is now bone of my bones and flesh of my flesh; she shall be called 'woman' for she was taken out of man." For this reason a man will leave his father and mother and be united to his wife, and they will become one flesh.*
>
> Gen. 2:21-24

Here is God's vision for marriage. He intended for a husband and wife to be united in committed love—a lifetime love. In the Genesis passage there is no exception. He didn't even mention adultery as a possibility. (Admittedly, Adam and Eve didn't have many opportunities for adultery!)

Years later when Moses speaks to Israel, however, the effects of sin are pervasive. Divorce was rampant not only in the ancient Near Eastern world but also, specifically, in Israel. So Moses' guidance wasn't to authorize divorce; rather, it was to mollify some of the ripping and tearing effects of divorce.

Some of the older translations of scripture (like the King James Version and the American Standard Version) make it difficult to understand what this text is doing. They make it sound as if the paragraph is full of commands. But newer translations help make it clear that following the hypothetical conditions ("If . . ."), there is only one command. Here are all the conditions that just describe what was already happening:

> If a man marries a woman who becomes displeasing to him because he finds something indecent about her, and he writes her a certificate of divorce, gives it to her and sends her from his house, and if after she leaves his house she becomes the wife of another man, and her second husband dislikes her and writes her a certificate of divorce, gives it to her and sends her from his house, or if he dies . . . .
>
> Deut. 24:1-3

If all that happens, then the regulation of verse 4 comes into force: "then her first husband, who divorced her, is not allowed to marry her again after she has been defiled."

The only command we have from Moses, then, is a protection for women. It is, in essence, an emancipation proclamation for the women of Israel. They weren't to be subjected to the whimsical, capricious desires of men. If a man put away his wife, she was free and protected.[2]

When the Pharisees asked Jesus about divorce, they showed that they didn't understand God's intentions. They wanted to know why Moses *commanded* a certificate of divorce. Jesus replied that Moses *permitted* it because of hard hearts. God sometimes permits in this fallen world something that is not his original desire.

The difference between the Pharisees and Jesus is stark: they read the Old Testament to justify divorce, and he read it to strengthen marriage. They understood Deuteronomy as a command to divorce; he saw it as a concession that would protect women.[3]

Lifelong Love

But the call of the good news of the kingdom is for a lifelong commitment. With the ripping and tearing of relationships all around, it is truly salt and light in a community when believers maintain their vows through good and bad days. It is a witness to the world of the rugged love of the One whose love has broken through.

I've seen believers work through emotional baggage, sexual problems, loss of dreams, challenges with children, and grief—all the while committed to maintaining their vows. I've witnessed older Christ-followers as they've walked their lifelong spouses through the dark fog of Alzheimer's.

Walter Wangerin has reflected back on the difficult times he and his wife have been through in marriage and of their devotion to the call of God as they endured those hard times:

> And the thing that neither one of us would even contemplate was divorce. We were stuck with each other. Let the world call that imprisonment; but I say it gave us the time, and God the opportunity, to make a better thing between us. If we could have escaped, we would have. Because we couldn't we were forced to choose the harder, better road.[4]

I used to hear that love holds our marriages together; perhaps it is even more true for Christians that our marital commitments hold our love together. (Of course, that's confusing, because *agape* love is a committed love.) This commitment says, "Because God is ruling, I will never leave you or forsake you."

To some who might think that's repressive, I'd insist that just the opposite is true. This kind of commitment is the only way for us to be freed to really love one another. We are not seeking for our spouse to meet our deepest needs. We know only God can do that. Therefore, we are freed to love one another with the love that serves, honors, submits, and endures.

Matthew 19:9 mentions an exception: "except for sexual immorality," Jesus says. But even this is a concession. My fear is that some might start playing the Pharisaic game all over again. At times the betrayal of sexual infidelity makes a coming together again impossible. But not necessarily! Many people of faith have—with patience, the help of friends, prayer, and forgiveness—seen their marriages restored, and at times even strengthened, following sexual immorality.

A stunning announcement came a few years ago. An influential Christian author and minister resigned "for personal reasons, having been involved in an adulterous relationship." He was repentant. His faith was still intact. But what about his marriage? Don't we usually assume divorce follows an admission of adultery, almost as automatically as winter follows autumn?

But in an interview shortly after the announcement, the man's wife asked people to remember that he'd been a person of integrity for the twenty-five years they had been married. Then she said—and let this sentence embed itself in your soul—"I will not dwell on that short period of time when he fell into sin."

"I will not dwell." Those words are set to the tune of three-part harmony: courage, freedom, and forgiveness. They are bold words that refuse to camp in the forest of bitterness.

I still love the note Charlie Shedd's wife left him on the refrigerator one day after they'd had a big argument: "Dear Charlie, I hate you. Love, Martha." That's the love that discipleship forms. No wonder these

words, originally penned to help a church battling selfish-
ness, have been spoken at so many Christian weddings:

*Love is patient, love is kind. It does not envy, it does
not boast, it is not proud. It does not dishonor others, it
is not self-seeking, it is not easily angered, it keeps no
record of wrongs. Love does not delight in evil but
rejoices with the truth. It always protects, always trusts,
always hopes, always perseveres. Love never fails.*

1 Cor. 13:4-8

Chapter 6
TRUTH IN A
PINOCCHIO WORLD

You have heard that it was said to the people long ago,
"Do not break your oath, but keep the oaths you have
made to the Lord." But I tell you, do not swear at all . . . .
—Matthew 5:33

D on't ask me why, but it seemed like a good idea at the time. With our children ages four and two, we decided to take them to Disney World. When I say *two*, I mean just barely two. Two by a few days. Megan, mentally-challenged but full of energy, had just had her birthday.

Here's what I wasn't prepared for. I knew it cost quite a bit (Can you say "understatement"?) for us to pass through the turnstile. But what I didn't know was that children under two were f-r-e-e. Gratis.

It was an all-or-nothing deal. If they are one year, 364 days, and twenty-three hours, they cost zip. An hour later, you have to take out a loan for the privilege of seeing Mickey and Minnie.

Temptation struck at this raw, penny-pinched nerve. No one would know! Besides, it was pretty clear looking around that other parents were claiming the deduction for kids who were a good bit older than

Megan. (I thought maybe the facial hair gave it away with one or two.)

Here was the really nasty part of the temptation: Megan had been born a month early. By God's plan, she should not have been two yet!

End of the story? I paid. But I can't say it felt good. I'm not sure about the whole "honesty is the best policy" motto. For real honesty, it's going to take something far better than "best policy."

Honest Ephahs, Honest Hins

What Jesus says the people had heard, "Do not break your oath, but keep the oaths you have made to the Lord," does not appear just like that in the Old Testament. It's more of a summary of several passage. For example, the third commandment forbids the using of God's name "in vain." That's probably not primarily referring to cursing. The loose, obscene way many use God's name is certainly wrong, but that's not the focus of the third commandment. It forbids perjury. We're told to honor God enough that when we invoke his name in an oath, we honor the pledge. We refuse to take his name lightly.

The holiness texts consistently call for honesty because of the nature of God. Integrity is one of many ways in which we're to be holy because our deliverer God is holy.

> Do not lie. Do not deceive one another. Do not swear falsely by my name and so profane the name of your God. I am the Lord. Do not defraud your neighbor or rob him.
>
> Lev. 19:11-13

Do not use dishonest standards when measuring length, weight or quantity. Use honest scales and honest weights, an honest ephah and an honest hin. I am the Lord your God, who brought you out of Egypt.
Lev. 19:35f

Moses' law unequivocally demanded honesty in all areas of life. God wants his people to honor their word. If an oath is called for, then the people of faith should carry through with the oath.

Pharisaic Corruption

In the Sermon on the Mount, Jesus attacks the Pharisees' bogus use of scripture that wound up circumventing God's intentions. You can tell by his words that the religious leaders had been making lots of oaths:

Do not swear at all: either by heaven, for it is God's throne; or by the earth, for it is his footstool, or by Jerusalem, for it is the city of the Great King. And do not swear by your head, for you cannot make even one hair white or black.
Matt. 5:34-36

It's perhaps hard for us to understand why they were swearing by heaven, earth, Jerusalem, or even their heads. But Jesus' third of seven woes upon the Pharisees in Matthew 23 offers some insight:

Woe to you, blind guides! You say, "If anyone swears by the temple, it means nothing; but whoever swears by the gold of the temple is bound by the oath." You blind fools! Which is greater: the gold, or the temple that makes the gold sacred? You also say, "If anyone swears by the altar, it means nothing; but whoever swears by the gift on the altar is bound by the oath." You blind

*men! Which is greater: the gift, or the altar that makes
the gift sacred? Therefore, anyone who swears by the
altar swears by it and by everything on it. And anyone
who swears by the temple swears by it and by the one
who dwells in it. And anyone who swears by heaven
swears by God's throne and by the one who sits on it.*

Matt. 23:16-22

Do you see how their oaths were a way of tap danc-
ing around the truth? Some oaths were considered binding; others weren't. If they said, "I swear by the temple
in Jerusalem," their word wasn't binding. But if they
said, "I swear by the gold in the temple," it was. An oath
based on an altar gift was binding; one based on the
altar itself wasn't. Apparently, the gold and the gift
carried more weight than the temple and the altar.
Doesn't that say something about their priorities?

The point, however, is that there were times when
they would take oaths and not honor them. It was their
equivalent of having their fingers crossed behind their
backs. If they swore by the temple, the altar, heaven,
the earth, or their own heads, they might not be telling
the "truth and nothing but the truth."

Out of all those Old Testament instructions on verac-
ity, they had seized upon the phrase "to the Lord." If
God's name was invoked, then honesty was demanded.
But otherwise, you couldn't count on what they said. So
even when they told the truth they were liars, because the
only truth they were committed to was convenient truth.

Modern Pharisaism

It was Diogenes who kept walking through the
streets of Athens looking for an honest man. He might
have a long walk in our culture today—a culture much
more at home with the Pharisees' shallow commitment

to truth. James Patterson and Peter Kim, in their book *The Day America Told the Truth*, put it baldly:

> *Americans lie. They lie more than we had ever thought possible before the study. But they told us the truth about how much they lie. Just about everyone lies—91 percent of us lie regularly. The majority of us find it hard to get through a week without lying.*[1]

Their study found half-truths, fibs, white lies, and whopping fabrications to be so deeply imbedded in our national character that they called it a "cultural trait." In the wake of huge corporate scandals in the early 21st century, it's easy to wonder if they were the exception or if they just got caught!

I spoke to a student recently at a Christian college who said she's been in several classes with a professor who will ask on an exam, "Did you read the assignments?" Students have told her that they routinely lie, figuring that if the professor is stupid enough to ask the question, they aren't obligated to be honest.

Before hammering them too hard, you have to wonder: Where did they learn such situational truth?

Most people don't seem to believe that honesty is always the "best policy." Isn't that why many employers have learned to discount ten to twenty percent of what they read on resumes? Could that be why it's become such a small thing to call in sick just to get a day off?

Some of the lies that swarm around us are just casual fibs:

> "The check is in the mail."
> "We service what we sell."
> "I just need a minute of your time."
> "No, you didn't wake me up."
> "I'll be praying for you."

Think of all the tolerated abuses. Padded billable hours. Abused expense funds. Slight omissions with the IRS. (I read that years ago the IRS received a note that said: "Gentlemen: Enclosed you'll find a check for $150. I cheated on my income tax return last year and have not been able to sleep ever since. If I still have trouble sleeping, I'll send you the rest.")

The problem is that if ethics are built only on "best policy," we will find many occasions when fibs, distortions, and fudging seem best.

Letting "Yes" and "No" Stand Alone

Jesus reads the Old Testament not to skirt around its clear call for honesty but to see what a heart shaped by the rule of God will look like. So he calls us to absolute truthfulness based on the nature of God and on the demands of discipleship. As people who believe the true word of God in Christ, we speak words of truth—regardless of whether it seems like the "best policy" in a moment of crisis.

We refuse to slide by with little lies at home to make the evening go smoother. ("I had to stay late at work." "You never told me that." "I didn't hear you.") We are unwilling to shape our image in untruthful ways, no matter how beneficial it might be at the office.

Jesus exposes the artificiality of their swearing. How can an oath to God be binding when an oath to heaven isn't? Doesn't God live in heaven? And doesn't God put his feet on earth? Isn't Jerusalem his city? Isn't he the one who changes the hair from black to white? (Grecian Formula takes it the other way!) The point of the law wasn't to become preoccupied with the formula "to the Lord," but to send us down paths of truth.

With all those games, Jesus says to quit making

oaths. His disciples simply need to say "yes" or "no" and let their word stand. His words are echoed by James:

> *Above all, my brothers and sisters, do not swear—not by heaven or by earth or by anything else. All you need to say is a simple "Yes" or "No." Otherwise you will be condemned.*
>
> James 5:12

You don't have to add to your simple words, because you are a person whose heart is truthful. You needn't say, "I swear on my Grandmother's grave" or "I swear on a stack of Bibles." As a Christ-follower, your word will stand alone. People will recognize that you don't dance around the truth.

There are people I know whose word I would never doubt. If you told me they had lied, I'd say, "You're mistaken." These are people who might be wrong, but they wouldn't intentionally mislead. Forget about swearing to heaven, earth, or Jerusalem. Their word sticks because their hearts have been changed inside out.

That's how it should be with all who follow him, Jesus says. When they call in sick, they're sick. When they report figures on their income tax returns, that information is correct (to the best of their knowledge). When they say they're out of the office, you can count on it.

Did Jesus absolutely forbid taking an oath in any situation? Some have believed, based on his words, that you cannot go into a court of law and take an oath to testify. But keep in mind Jesus' context. He wasn't addressing the question, "Can a Christian ever swear an oath in a court of law?" Rather than anticipating every situation that might come up, he was attacking religious liars who hid behind half-truths.

If Jesus was forbidding ever taking an oath, we run into problems later in Matthew's gospel. Jesus had been silent before the authorities, but now the high priest challenged him: "I charge you under oath by the living God: Tell us if you are the Christ, the Son of God." Jesus didn't refuse to answer. He didn't say, "I'm sorry, I never take oaths." He replied, "Yes, it is as you say" (Matt. 26:63f). In that judicial setting, he did take an oath before God. But it wasn't because his integrity could be questioned. He was the model: If he said "yes," you could take it to the bank. If he said "no," you knew he meant it.

A Daily Test

The "honesty is the best policy" line goes back to Cervantes. But for Christians, this isn't our utilitarian motto. Honesty isn't just the best policy. It is God's policy. He's a God who cannot lie, and it's incumbent upon us to reflect his truthful nature.

One time as a wise teacher passed out a trigonometry test, he said, "I'm giving you two tests today: one in trigonometry and one in honesty. I hope you pass both of them. But if you pass only one, be sure it's the test in honesty, because there are a lot of good people who don't know any trigonometry, but there are no good people who are not honest."

As seekers of God, we take that test daily. We choose each day to let his will flow through us, refusing to play Pharisaic games. Our "yes" means yes; our "no" means no. We rise above the fib-infested waters around us.

Chapter 7
LOOK AT JESUS ONLY

You have heard that it was said, "Eye for eye, and tooth for tooth." But I tell you, do not resist an evil person.
—Matthew 5:38

A man was driving home after work, disconcerted by all the construction surrounding him on the tollway. He cell phone rang, and when he answered it he heard the agitated voice of his wife. "Honey, be careful. I just heard on the radio that there's a car going the wrong direction on the tollway." He said, "It's not just one! There are hundreds of them!"

All of Jesus' examples so far have gone upstream. But this one is so counter-cultural you'll wonder if you're going the wrong direction.

After the heinous attacks of September 11, 2001, there was a response that probably could have been predicted. Many Americans of Middle Eastern descent were attacked. Some verbally; others physically. It wasn't much different from the kind of treatment Asian-American citizens received when they were persecuted during the years of the Second World War.

Victims seek revenge. As W. H. Auden's simple rhyme suggests:

> I and the public know
> What all school children learn—
> Those to whom evil is done
> Do evil in return.

Part of why movies like *Unforgiven* (1992), *Braveheart* (1995), and *The Patriot* (2000) do so well at the box office is that people can identify with the desire to even a score. Revenge plays well! A dark part of each of us relishes the words "eye for eye, tooth for tooth." Like Shylock, we demand a pound of flesh for the injuries we've suffered.

The dark cloud of retaliation hovers over many American families. Millions each year are assaulted by members of their own family. Eye for eye.

Someone cuts in front of you in traffic, causing you to hit the brakes. You've been insulted! Nothing would feel better than to quickly even that score with a horn or an obscene gesture. Tooth for tooth.

Since we've been injured, we convince ourselves that our revenge is a "righteous revenge." This attitude provides a high-octane fuel that can burn longer and hotter, allowing us to lash out viciously at educators, politicians, the media, parents, children, siblings, competitors, spouses, bosses, church leaders, friends, and strangers.

You pat me on the back, and I'll return the favor. But if you insult me, expect an insult in return. Isn't that expected?

A blind man was working his way through busy traffic with his seeing-eye dog when the dog led him into a dangerous situation, nearly getting him killed. Horns were blaring all around him. Immediately he went home and gave his dog a big bowl of food. His friends said they couldn't believe his magnanimous spirit. "Why would you do that? He nearly got you killed?" He answered, "I'm going to find out which end he eats with and then kick his teeth out!"

There it is: eye for eye, tooth for tooth.

Scriptural Arsenal

Jesus tells his followers that they'd heard "eye for eye and tooth for tooth." This wasn't just a saying of the Pharisees, however; it was straight out of the scripture of Israel. Read carefully these passages from the Torah and imagine how they might have stoked the Pharisees' desire for revenge:

> *If men who are fighting hit a pregnant woman and she gives birth prematurely but there is no serious injury, the offender must be fined whatever the woman's husband demands and the court allows. But if there is serious injury, you are to take life for life, eye for eye, tooth for tooth, hand for hand, foot for foot, burn for burn, wound for wound, bruise for bruise.*
>
> Ex. 21:22-25

> *If anyone injures his neighbor, whatever he has done must be done to him: fracture for fracture, eye for eye, tooth for tooth. As he has injured the other, so he is to be injured.*
>
> Lev. 24:19

> *Show no pity: life for life, eye for eye, tooth for tooth, hand for hand, foot for foot.*
>
> Deut. 19:21

People with a taste for retaliation didn't have to search very hard to find their proof texts. It was there in black and white.

How Jesus Read the Law

But keep in mind that Jesus all along has been affirming Moses, not countering him. So what we'd expect to find here—and I think that's just what we have—is not Jesus upending the law of Moses but Jesus showing how the religious leaders had misinterpreted Moses.

When he read scripture, he didn't understand "eye for eye, tooth for tooth" the way the Pharisees did. He knew that God, who had been as concerned about the heart with Israel as he was now, had not allowed a free-for-all environment of retaliation.

He doesn't explain here just how he read the law differently, but we can make a couple of reasonable inferences. First, he understood that the "law of retaliation" involved courts in Israel. Those who had committed a crime had to be punished because of their violation of the sanctity of life. But the administration of justice was a matter for the courts. This reflects not a disregard for life but a very high value for life.

Moses, then, didn't sanction vigilante justice where *you* go after the eye, the tooth, the foot, or the hand. It doesn't deputize you to head out like Clint Eastwood ready to even a score.

Even the New Testament speaks about the authority God has given to government to carry out punishment against evildoers.

> Let everyone be subject to the governing authorities, for there is no authority except that which God has established. The authorities that exist have been established by God. Consequently, whoever rebels against the authority is rebelling against what God has instituted, and those who do so will bring judgment on themselves. For rulers hold no terror for those who do right, but for those who do wrong. Do you want to be free from fear of the one

in authority? Then do what is right and you will be commended. For the one in authority is God's servant for your good. But if you do wrong, be afraid, for rulers do not bear the sword for no reason. They are God's servants, agents of wrath to bring punishment on the wrongdoer. Therefore, it is necessary to submit to the authorities, not only because of possible punishment but also as a matter of conscience.

Rom. 13:1-5

Without punishment by government, we'd be left with anarchy. And it is God's high esteem for life and the value of every human being that causes him to endorse this system of punishment: not vigilante justice, but a system of courts and law.

Jesus also understood that there is tremendous grace and protection even in the law of retaliation. For rarely do we just try to even the score. If someone rudely brushes against your shoulder, what's the first urge? Well, to do something considerably worse than returning the brush! The human tendency would be "head for eye" rather than "eye for eye."

Years ago when Diane and I moved to Memphis, the first night was a bit scary for us. We'd never lived in a city even nearly that size. To be honest, the biggest "city" I'd ever lived in had about 10,000 people. So, with images of crime in our heads, we purchased all the security locks we thought our little apartment could stand. We locked the windows. And we locked the locks that locked the windows.

Our first evening there, as we walked out I was attacked by a dog. All right, not a huge Rottweiler or anything. It was one of those little weenie dogs. As he nipped at me, I began kicking toward him. I wasn't trying to bash his head in; I was just trying to avoid being bitten.

Out of nowhere came a huge hulk of a man, barreling out of his truck. He pointed his finger at me and screamed, "You kick my dog again and I'll blow your head off!"

Now, it would have taken a really stupid person to do that . . . but he appeared to have all the credentials! As I thought about it later, he was going way beyond the law of retaliation. That would demand, "You kick my dog again, and I'll go kick your dog." Ha! I didn't even have a dog. But it wasn't my pet he threatened; it was my head on a platter.

Human inclination seeks the jugular. Someone has ripped you off, hurting your reputation and your business. The pound you want in return isn't British money but flesh.

So perhaps there is a touch of mercy deep within this law—protection for people who might otherwise have been hurt unjustly by human overreaction and vengeance.

Blessing Those Who Curse

Regarding personal injuries, Jesus tells us that what God has always wanted is for people with kingdom hearts to repay evil with good, to repay cursing with blessing. When someone strikes us on the cheek we're to turn the other, refusing to strike back.

Several years ago, we were in St. Louis right after twenty inches of snow. We had just met a couple from a church where I was speaking. As we pulled into a shopping strip, this church leader parked as best he could. With that much snow, it's tough to see the thin parking lines.

Just as we were getting out, some gruff old goat began pounding on the car window and screaming:

"Why can't you learn to park!" Apparently we were taking up a couple spaces, and it had caused him to walk a few extra steps.

I was much younger (in my defense—if this is any defense!), but my first thought was, "Let's beat the stuffings out of this old coot! He's an idiot." But immediately, before he had a chance to think about the presence of a young minister and his wife in the back seat (since most of us can behave well if we think about who's looking), he responded: "Yes, sir. Thanks for telling me. I'll try again."

It was a stunning lesson I'll never forget. With a heart wildly passionate about the rule of God, he had no interest in straightening someone out or in evening a score. No eye for eye. No tooth for tooth. No scream for scream.

This is rugged discipleship here, my friends. When somebody injures you, your human nature wants to bite their neck and watch them bleed to death. (I have this fear that you're thinking, "They let this guy write a Christian book?")

Jesus offers four examples of what this spirit of mercy looks like in action. First, "if someone slaps you on the right cheek, turn to them the other cheek also" (v. 39). Second, "if anyone wants to sue you and take your shirt, hand over your coat as well" (v. 40). Third, "if anyone forces you to go one mile, go with them two miles" (v. 41) And fourth, "give to the one who asks you, and do not turn away from the one who wants to borrow from you" (v. 42).

In each of these examples, someone is trying to inflict harm. Jesus pleads with you, "Don't retaliate!" Be careful not to read these instructions with a wooden literalism. We've already seen how he makes use of hyperbole (e.g., "gouge [your eye] out and throw it away") throughout the message.

But in running from wooden literalism, we must not undermine the radical voice of Christ. We are not to be people who worry about leveling all scores. We are not to return injury for injury.

Look Only At Jesus

Corrie ten Boom, having witnessed the constant ridicule of her sister, Betsie, by prison guards in a Nazi concentration camp, had seen all she could endure. She watched in horror as a guard took a leather strip and slashed Betsie across her chest and neck.

Flushed with red-hot anger, Corrie grabbed a shovel and rushed the guard. But she was intercepted by her sister, whose collar was turning crimson from the cut. Betsie pleaded with her to keep working. She covered the whip mark Corrie was staring at and said gently but firmly, "Don't look at it, Corrie. Look at Jesus only."

That's just how the early Christians were encouraged to think and respond when they were insulted. The book of 1 Peter was apparently written, for example, to believers who were been mocked, insulted, and scorned. They were told to "not repay evil with evil or insult with insult" (1 Pet. 3:9).

But that command was anchored in the life of Jesus. Peter said to his fellow believers, in essence: "look at Jesus only." To the slaves among them he wrote:

Slaves, in reverent fear of God submit yourselves to your masters, not only to those who are good and considerate, but also those who are harsh. For it is commendable if you bear up under the pain of unjust suffering because you are conscious of God. But how is it to your credit if you receive a beating for doing wrong and endure it? But if you suffer for doing good and you endure it, this is commendable before God. To this you were called, because Christ suffered for you, leaving you an example that you should follow in his steps. "He committed no sin, and no deceit was found in his mouth." When they hurled their insults at him, he did not retaliate; when he suffered, he made no threat. Instead, he entrusted himself to him who judges justly.

1 Pet. 2:18-23

Keep your eyes only on Jesus. When they spat at him, he didn't spit back. When they insulted him, he didn't return the favor. When they beat him, he didn't strike them dead. He responded to evil with good. That's the strength of a devoted kingdom person. They're able to take an injustice and walk away, refusing to even the score.

The decision to follow Jesus is a risky one. Pharisaic righteousness is much safer. All the messages around us—warnings of politicians, opinions of radio personalities, prime time programs, movies, magazine articles—tell us that the way ahead is "eye for eye, tooth for tooth."

Don't believe them! Look only at Jesus.

Chapter 8
LOVE OF
ANOTHER KIND

You have heard that it was said, "Love your neighbor
and hate your enemy." But I tell you: Love your
enemies and pray for those who persecute you.
—Matthew. 5:43

I don't remember a lot of things about when I was six years old, but there's one thing I recall almost as if it happened yesterday. My grandma and aunt took me to Kansas City to watch "Peter Pan" in an outdoor theater. This special aunt who was closer to my age had doted on me all the time. As we went into the outdoor theater they bought me a laser gun that was equipped with fantastic noises and flashing lights. And on the side it had numbers one, two, three, four, and five that you could punch.

I asked what the numbers were for, and my aunt explained, "Well, they're degrees of intensity. Don't ever push number five, because it would melt someone right where they are. You can push one, two, three—four— maybe, but don't ever press five." I carefully set it at one or two and tucked it away, and we began watching "Peter Pan."

At intermission my aunt took me to the restroom. But in a big place like that, where do you send a six-year-old boy? You don't dare send him into the men's restroom. Who knows what might happen without supervision in there? So she took me into the ladies' room. I thought nothing about it. I was just following this aunt who loved me.

Then suddenly, a little brunette about my age, three feet high with a mouth four feet wide, began screaming, "There's a boy in the girls' bathroom!" My face flushed. It suddenly hit me. I was not where I should be. We didn't do it that way at first grade. We had no unisex restrooms. I was in the wrong place, and suddenly it felt like I was in a whole room of amazon women—women who were staring at me while this little girl continued shooting her mouth off, "There's a boy in the girls' bathroom!"

I didn't know what to do. So I pulled out that laser gun, put it on five, and shot her! Immediately, my aunt rushed me out of there. I still don't know if she melted.

From the Difficult to the Unreal

In commanding us to love our enemies—even little girls who embarrass us in public restrooms—Jesus passes from the difficult to the unreal. Love your enemies?

The Pharisees about whom Jesus spoke in Matthew 5:20 and throughout the Sermon on the Mount understood well that it's easy to love those who love you and to greet those who greet you, but that it's very hard to love your enemies. Did the Pharisees love anyone? Of course they did. They loved other Pharisees. Did they love other Jews of the land? Well, usually. Despite some differences, they might even love a Sadducee now and then. But what about all the slimy Samaritans, tawdry tax collectors and galling Gentiles, especially those who dared to occupy the land in the name of Rome? How do you love someone like that?

Jesus said, "You've heard it said that you should love your neighbor and hate your enemy." Does that come out of the Old Testament? Well, yes and no. Leviticus 19 was the golden text for the Pharisees. It says, "Do not seek revenge or bear a grudge against one of your people, but love your neighbor as yourself. I am the Lord."

Their commentary on that was that since you were supposed to love your neighbor, the obvious implication was that you were to hate your enemy. Otherwise, why would God say to love your neighbor? (Isn't that how we often reason?) So they had a text. Religious tyrants with texts can be very scary!

It wasn't a very full reading of Leviticus 19, however, as we can see:

> When you reap the harvest of your land, do not reap to the very edges of your field or gather the gleanings of your harvest. Do not go over your vineyard a second time or pick up the grapes that have fallen. Leave them for the poor and the alien. I am the Lord your God ... When an alien lives with you in your land, do not mistreat him. The alien living with you must be treated as one of your native-born. Love him as yourself, for you were aliens in Egypt. I am the Lord your God.
> Lev.19:9-10, 33-34

But if you're trying to prove something, you don't have to read every verse, do you? If you want to argue that loving your neighbor means hating your enemy, you just skip some of those verses and focus on the phrase you want.

Most of us find it fairly easy to love those who love us, who bolster our self-esteem, who make us feel good about ourselves. But that's the kind of Pharisaic love Jesus was talking about, the kind of love that will only appreciate and act kindly toward those who love us.

That was the provincial love of Jonah. He was called by God to go preach to the Assyrians. Now, if you were an Israelite prophet, there was no one you'd rather condemn than the Assyrians. But Jonah knew he couldn't trust God to be unmerciful. So what did he do? He went the other way. But God had a way of calling him back. Jonah was cast into the water and swallowed by a big fish. The big fish then spit him up, proving, as the song says, "You can't keep a good man down." And there was Jonah, sent again to Nineveh.

In Luke 9, Jesus was on his way to Jerusalem, and he was going to pass through Samaria. He didn't have to, but he was going to. Some messengers went on ahead to see if everything was ready for the Master, and they reported, "Hey, the Samaritans don't want you to pass through because you're going to Jerusalem." Now you get James and John, Sons of Thunder, in the picture, and they said, "Lord, you want us to call down fire from heaven?" Just bring it down and zap them right there!

How would that feel? Have you ever thought that about anyone? Secretly now, have you ever wanted to just call down fire from heaven?

How can you possibly love someone at school who has circulated trashy rumors about you so that people are starting to avoid you? How do you love someone at work who tried to get you fired because your hard work was an indictment of her laziness? How do you love someone who insults your spouse publicly or harasses one of your children—maybe a coach who convinces your boy he's a no-good klutz? Or imagine a rape victim as she's lying on a hospital bed with her jaw wired shut and her ribs broken, thinking about her attacker. Suppose you're the parent of a fourteen-year-old boy whose life has just been snuffed out by a drunk driver who walked away from both the wreck and the courts unscathed. How do you love?

Picture the college girl who cries herself to sleep every night thinking about a stepfather who abused her. Or maybe the enemy is a landlord who's eager to take your money but slow to fix anything. It could be that boy who made your daughter feel horrible about herself before breaking off the relationship. It could be that boss who seems to be harder on you than on any other employee, those in-laws who have always made you feel inadequate, that neighbor who lets his dog howl all night long, those church leaders who are overly judgmental, or that teacher who lied to you about what would be covered on the final exam. Such people ought to be corralled and shot, don't you think?

Natural human love is geared to those who are lovely, who are like us. We want to love those who love us and greet those who greet us. But Jesus calls for more. If those are the only people we love, what have we done more than others? But it's a different kind of love to which Jesus calls us.

Frederick Buechner wrote in his book *The Magnificent Defeat:*

> *The love for equals is a human thing—of friend for friend, brother for brother. It is to love what is loving and lovely. The world smiles.*
>
> *The love for the less fortunate is a beautiful thing—the love for those who suffer, for those who are poor, the sick, the failures, the unlovely. This is compassion, and it touches the heart of the world.*
>
> *The love for the more fortunate is a rare thing—to love*

those who succeed where we fail, to rejoice without envy with those who rejoice, the love of the poor for the rich, of the black man for the white man. The world is always bewildered by its saints.

And then there is the love for the enemy—love for the one who does not love you but mocks, threatens, and inflicts pain. The tortured's love for the torturer. This is God's love. It conquers the world.[1]

Love of Another Kind

The command to love our enemies is the sixth example in Matthew 5 of that righteousness which comes from inside—the righteousness that surpasses that of the Pharisees and teachers of the law. Jesus enters that tender little chamber of our lives where grudges are fed and watered. Love your neighbor, but love your enemy also.

I tell you, love your enemies and pray for those who persecute you, that you may be children of your Father in heaven. He causes his sun to rise on the evil and the good, and sends rain on the righteous and the unrighteous. If you love those who love you, what reward will you get? Are not even the tax collectors doing that? And if you greet only your own people, what are you doing more than others? Do not even pagans do that?

Matt. 5:44-47

The word "surpasses" from verse 20 is the same root word found in verse 47 when Jesus fleshes out the concept of loving enemies. As people who've been dramatically altered by the kingdom of God, we're to go beyond shallow definitions of love. There's no room for vindictiveness with our enemies. We're to love them. It's an across-the-board kind of love. So how do you do that with someone you'd just as soon choke as look at?

Let's begin with the kind of love he was talking about. Feelings are so hard to control, aren't they? Sometimes even when I want to do right, I can't control my feelings. But he wasn't talking about feelings. The only kind of love we can command is some kind of action, of decision, of commitment. It's a resolve that says I'm going to act in the best interest of that person. This doesn't give us the right to have feelings of hatred toward people; it's just the basic recognition that we can't control all those feelings. It's hard to feel bad about somebody toward whom you're acting lovingly, however.

C. S. Lewis said of this kind of love, "It doesn't mean an emotion. It is a state, not of the feelings, but of the will." And New Testament scholar C. H. Dodd, in his book *Gospel and Law*, said this love ". . . is not primarily an emotion or an affection. It is primarily an act of determination of the will. That is why it can be commanded as feelings cannot."

There are three qualities of this *agape* love we're commanded to have. One is that it's unmotivated. It doesn't depend on what the other person has done for us. The motive is God's graciousness toward us.

Second, it's nonselective. It doesn't go around like a heat-seeking missile, looking for a particular target. It's across the board. It's to those who are like us and those who aren't, to those who like us and those who hate us.

Third, it's unilateral. It doesn't demand anything in return. We commit to love others whether they respond with a bouquet of flowers or a mouthful of spit.

How do we put that kind of love into practice? Jesus offers us the place to begin by commanding us to pray for our enemies. It is hard to stoke the flames of hatred for people whose names you're lifting up in intercession.

Is that really possible? Ask Elisabeth Elliot as she cuts the hair of one of the men who murdered her husband as he went out to preach to them in Ecuador. Ask a rape victim I know who has prayed every day for her attacker. Ask Jesus in that upper room as he kneels down to wash Judas's feet. Ask them if it's possible.

Jesus gave the kingdom motive for this kind of love: "that you may be children of your Father in heaven." Quit looking at the world and start looking at the Father.

How does the Father act? "He causes his sun to rise on . . . the good." Yes, on the good, but the complete phrase says "on the evil and the good." What about the rain? Does it come down on the righteous? Yes. But it also comes down on the unrighteous. Many of God's blessings are available to all. He gives because he loves to give. The rain and the sun are there for everyone, whether a person responds in love to God or not. He's still the author of blessings.

The most concrete example of loving the unlovely was the cross. Paul captured the power of Calvary's love with these words:

> *You see, at just the right time, when we were still powerless, Christ died for the ungodly. Very rarely will anyone die for a righteous person, though for a good person someone might possibly dare to die. But God demonstrates his own love for us in this: While we were still sinners, Christ died for us. Since we have now been justified by his blood, how much more shall we be saved from God's wrath through him! For if, while we were God's enemies, we were reconciled to him through the death of his Son, how much more, having been reconciled, shall we be saved through his life!*
> Rom. 5:6-10

That's the supreme example of what Jesus was talking about in the Sermon on the Mount. We were enemies of God. We were powerless sinners. Yet that's when Christ died for us. That's when the Father sent his Son into the world to die for that world.

There are a lot of things we can't know about our enemies. But three truths are certain: (1) they were made in the image of God; (2) Christ died for them; (3) God loves each of them as much as he loves us.

Called to Be Perfect

That leads us finally to verse 48, a tricky little verse at the end of this paragraph: "Be perfect, therefore, as your heavenly Father is perfect." That can be a real source of guilt if you understand it as a demand for moral perfection.

A better approach, however, is to interpret it in the context of the paragraph in which it's found. There it refers not to absolute moral perfection but to the kind of perfection Jesus called for throughout the paragraph. "Be perfect, therefore," he said, linking it to what he has just said. And what kind of perfection has he just called for? A complete, full, mature, God-formed kind of love.

Look at the Pharisee's love. They rained down on the righteous, but they withheld their rain from the unrighteous. Their sun shone on the good but was withheld from the evil. God doesn't do that. The sun comes down on everyone. The rain comes down on all people. God loves everyone! So Jesus insists that we be complete in our love as our heavenly Father is complete in his love—not stingy, not selective, but loving enemies as well as neighbors. In that sense, we're to be perfect as our heavenly Father is perfect. Then, as Jesus said in verse 45, we will truly be children of our Father in heaven.

The world's broken record keeps playing something like this: "Retaliate! Eye for eye, tooth for tooth. Love your neighbor. Hate your enemy. Retaliate. Eye for eye, tooth for tooth. Love your neighbor. Hate your enemy." It plays over and over again.

But Jesus asks us to swim upstream, to offer a love that is counter-cultural and heroic—the kind that comes only through the power of the Holy Spirit as we choose to let the Spirit form us in the ways of God. It's such a unique kind of love. In fact, it's so incredible that it becomes a convincing argument for our faith. Jesus said that by this kind of love, "people will know you are my disciples."

Chapter 9
AN AUDIENCE OF ONE

*Be careful not to do your "acts of righteousness" in front of
others, to be seen by them. If you do, you will have
no reward from your Father in heaven.*
—Matthew. 6:1

J esus has now illustrated six times what a kingdom-
shaped heart looks like. It isn't a shiny, polished
outside he's concerned with; it's a heart passionately
devoted to God.

Now he turns to a temptation that will always place
more focus on the outside than on the inside: the temptation to gain the approval of others. Later in Matthew's
gospel, he will warn in unmistakable words about the
Pharisees' attempts to be noticed by others:

*Everything they do is done for people to see: They
make their phylacteries wide and the tassels on their
garments long; they love the place of honor at
banquets and the most important seats in the synagogues; they love to be greeted with respect in the
marketplaces and to have people call them "Rabbi."*
Matt. 23:5-7

Notice how different their eagerness for public approval was from the Apostle Paul's insistence that he cared very little what others thought of him, as long as his audience of one was satisfied (1 Cor. 4:1-5).

It's a battle most of us face constantly. We want others to like us, to think we're bright and witty, to enjoy our company—in short, to approve of us. The writings of Henri Nouwen are filled with his attempts to break free from his inclination to be a people-pleaser. He wrote frankly in a journal, "For as long as you can remember, you have been a pleaser, depending on others to give you an identity."[1]

Jesus makes it clear that kingdom-shaped hearts don't worry about titles, about impressions, and about approval. They seek only the applause of God. So, he said, "Be careful not to do your 'acts of righteousness' in front of others, to be seen by them." The motive is important in this sentence. It isn't so much a question of how public or private we are—though he's going to advocate the discipline of secrecy—but what our intents are. Are we doing righteous deeds to be seen and approved by others, or are we doing them because our hearts are devoted to God?

Three Examples

The Pharisees wanted the accolades of the crowd. They wanted standing ovations as they took spiritual victory laps—ovations that recognized all they were doing for God.

This problem is spotlighted with three examples. First, Jesus mentions their propensity for putting price tags on all their gifts: "So when you give to the needy, do not announce it with trumpets, as the hypocrites do in the synagogues and on the streets, to be honored by others" (Matt. 6:2). The impact of Jesus' choice of words to describe the Pharisees is captured by Dallas Willard:

A special word about "the hypocrites" is required here. It is a term used by Jesus alone in the New Testament, and he uses it seventeen times. The term hypocrite in classical Greek primarily refers to an actor, such as one sees on the stage, but it came to refer also to anyone who practices deceit. It is clear from the literary records that it was Jesus alone who brought this term and the corresponding character into the moral vocabulary of the Western World. He did so because of his unique emphasis upon the moral significance of the inmost heart before God. As we are creative beings, our heart is who we really are. Jesus therefore made repeated and unmistakable distinctions between our face to the world and our person before God.[2]

It isn't the giving of alms that disturbs Jesus. He, after all, is the one who continually urged people to share God's passionate concern for social justice, for helping people in need.

It was the form and motive that concerned him. Their giving was heralded by trumpeters who called out, in essence: "Watch! Watch! This man of God is about to give! He's pulling out the checkbook! Watch carefully now because he's writing a check—undoubtedly a big check! Now look carefully as he places it in the collection tray!"

Jesus next exposed their attention-seeking prayers: "And when you pray, do not be like the hypocrites, for they love to pray standing in the synagogues and on the street corners to be seen by others" (Matt. 6:5). Why pray if no one knows about it? Why pray in a room with the shades drawn and the door closed? What's the point?

Exactly. "They have received their reward in full." They sought the attention, approval, and accolades of people and had received them. So what other reward would fit?

The third illustration of their hypocritical acts of righteousness was their practice of fasting. "When you fast, do not look somber as the hypocrites do, for they disfigure their faces to show others they are fasting" (Matt. 6:16). Be sure you understand that it isn't fasting (any more than giving or praying) that Jesus assails. Going without food can be a way to discipline the body so God can fill you. It can be the healthy "mortification of the flesh" that leads to greater dependence on God.

But it can also be an attention-getting device. Since the Pharisees were fasting for people to notice, they went out of their way to disfigure their faces so people would say: "My, that is one holy man of God! I'll bet he's been fasting for a month."

The Danger

When the religious leaders gave, it wasn't because their hearts were tuned to God's concern for the poor. When they prayed, it wasn't because they sought time with their heavenly Father. When they fasted, it wasn't to discipline their bodies in order to open their hearts more to the reign of God. Jesus' condemnation was consistent with the harsh words of the prophets before him.

Eight centuries before Christ, God said through Isaiah:

> Stop bringing meaningless offerings! Your incense is detestable to me. New Moons, Sabbaths, and convocations—I cannot bear your evil assemblies. Your New Moon festivals and your appointed feasts my soul hates. They have become a burden to me; I am weary of bearing them. When you spread out your hands in prayer, I

will hide my eyes from you; even if you offer many prayers, I will not listen. Your hands are full of blood; wash and make yourselves clean. Take your evil deeds out of my sight! Stop doing wrong, learn to do right! Seek justice, encourage the oppressed. Defend the cause of the fatherless, plead the case of the widow.

Isa. 1:13-17

Isaiah was telling the people of God: "He won't take that. He doesn't want to witness your fasting, your giving, your praying, your assembling—unless you have made a prior decision to seek him, to be conformed to his values, to worship him alone. Show him your just hearts; then let the religious acts follow."

In the same century, the prophet Amos also spoke for God:

I hate, I despise your religious feasts; I cannot stand your assemblies. Even though you bring me burnt offerings and grain offerings, I will not accept them. Though you bring choice fellowship offerings, I will have no regard for them. Away with the noise of your songs! I will not listen to the music of your harps. But let justice roll on like a river, righteousness like a never-failing stream!

Amos 5:21-24

Don't bother singing. Don't bother prayer. Forget your offerings. First, God says, your hearts need to be broken and restored with an interest in justice. He will not tolerate show-and-tell religion.

Not So Amusing

This is a good text to appreciate from a distance. As John Stott has written: "It is easy to poke fun at those Jewish Pharisees of the first century. Our Christian pharisaism is not so amusing."[3]

It isn't at all amusing! Would Jesus be as bothered when our religion becomes showy and ostentatious? Wouldn't we—like the Pharisees—insist that our motives have been misunderstand? It does raise some questions, though, doesn't it?

A friend of mine was in a large city and found himself behind a vehicle with an old "Honk if you love Jesus" bumper-sticker. So he honked. The driver turned around and began screaming something at him. Thankfully, he couldn't hear everything, but it seemed clear that it wasn't a Christian witness!

Do we launch into mission works because we have hearts like God—hearts that beat for lost people—or because we want to be seen as mission churches? Is it appropriate for churches to make sure their special contributions and their ministry programs are covered by newspapers (public or Christian)—or does that raise questions about our motives?

I'm thankful to minister at a church where the leaders have long had a policy that we'll keep our good deeds out of the local paper if at all possible. Our desire is to minister to the community in the name of Jesus—not to be KNOWN as a church that does certain things. People will know, of course. They'll see your good deeds and praise your Father in heaven (Matt. 5:16), but it won't be because you've become your own publicity firm. Jesus invites you to shine your light—not to turn the floodlights onto yourself!

The real battle we're waging is against pride, which seeks—either outright or through false humility—to receive those floodlights.

The Danish philosopher Soren Kierkegaard noted that too many Christians seem to think the preacher is on the stage performing, while they, the audience, are entertained. But, he said, that's not the flow of true worship at all. God is always the audience—the audience of one. The worship leader is just the conductor, and the members are the performers. We perform for him, not to be seen by men and women and certainly not to congratulate ourselves.

So Jesus advises us to give in a way that our left hand doesn't know what our right hand is doing. Some have taken this literally and sewn pieces of cloth over the collection plate so their right hand could give without the left hand seeing. (Can a left hand actually see?) But that misses the point, turning this into a quirky legalism. The obvious hyperbole underscores his point: that our acts of righteousness are for God.

What about prayer? In a similar vein, Jesus instructs: "When you pray, go into your room, close the door and pray to your Father, who is unseen." Again, we must not miss his point. It isn't the specific place that's important. You could, after all, go into your room and pray with the wrong motives. Can't you imagine someone saying, "Excuse me everyone. I'll be gone the next couple hours. I'll be in my room praying."

And fasting? "When you fast, put oil on your head and wash your face, so that it will not be obvious to others that you are fasting, but only to your Father, who is unseen." Do something so people won't gawk at you. Put on some make-up. Shave your face. Comb your hair. Let your fasting be between you and God. Let God—not others with their nodding approval—provide the proper reward.

Like Our Father

As much as God wants us to give, pray and properly fast, he doesn't need our money, our prayers, or our fasting. He wants us. The God who made us to be in community with himself—even as he, the Triune God, exists in perpetual community—longs for our hearts to be fully devoted to him.

Note the number of times the phrase "your Father" occurs in Matthew 6:1-18:

v. 1 – "If you do, you will have no reward from your Father in heaven."

v. 4 – "Then your Father, who sees what is done in secret, will reward you."

v. 6 – "Close the door and pray to your Father."

v. 8 – "Do not be like them, for your Father knows what you need."

v. 9 – "Our Father in heaven."

The word "Father" appears ten times in this little section, because this intimate relationship with our Father is the moving force behind all acts of right living. We give to the poor because we have been taught by our Father to care for all people—especially for the poor. We pray because we believe that our Father seeks communion with us. And we fast because we know our Father longs to transform us into the image of his Son.

Praying for Reign

My history with "the Lord's Prayer" is pretty checkered. Though I grew up in a church that taught it is wrong to pray the Lord's Prayer today (long story—see endnote!),[4] we did recite the prayer before our high school football games. The whole team would gather in a circle and pray, ending with "thine is the kingdom and the power and the glory forever. Amen." Then a few seconds later, we'd start chanting, "Kill them. Kill them. Kill them."

I'm thankful now to preach for a church that says the prayer together each week. Often I remind them that our voices are lifted up with Christ-followers from around the world—some meeting in sanctuaries, some gathering under trees, and some huddled in prisons—to pray:

Our Father who art in heaven,
Hallowed be thy name.
Thy kingdom come,
thy will be done
on earth as it is in heaven.
Give us this day our daily bread.
And forgive us our debts,
as we forgive our debtors.
And lead us not into temptation,
but deliver us from evil.
For thine is the kingdom,
and the power, and the glory,
forever. Amen.

This is a prayer without all the fat. It is slim, trim, to the point. It is, as Dallas Willard has aptly put it, the disciple's prayer, which has "an absolutely vital role in kingdom living."[5]

In this context, Jesus' central focus is on the pray-er. Prayer is meant to be an outgrowth of a heart that longs to be like the Father. The saying of this prayer is a discipline by which we come to know God more and more and by which we offer ourselves to him day by day.

Praying to Our Father

As we saw above, Jesus continually calls God "our Father." For many of the Jews in his day, God had become quite remote. They hadn't seen him act in a long time. They could read about his great actions from the past in the Old Testament, but where had he been for the past four centuries?

Some of the leaders developed a theological outlook that taught that there would be only one final, cataclysmic action of God and that other than this action in the future he isn't too involved. The Sadducees, for example, were practically deists. But beyond them, many Jews thought God was so remote, so removed, so ethereal that they could not even say his holy name. When they read the holy scrolls and came to the tetragrammaton, the four Hebrew letters that we might have translated "Jehovah" or "Yahweh," they wouldn't even say it. They would speak another word, *Adonai* ("Lord"). He was too far removed to even say his name.

You can almost feel the shock waves, then, when Jesus said to pray, "Our Father . . . ." Undoubtedly he was using the Aramaic word *abba*, an intimate endearing word (used also by Paul in Romans 8:15 and Galatians 4:6).

I love the prayer of the child who was asked in Bible class to quote the opening of the Lord's Prayer. She said, "Our Father who art in heaven, how do you know my name?" That's not a bad paraphrase! God is so almighty, so holy, and yet he knows me.

William Barclay relates an old Roman legend of an emperor returning from victory with the spoils of war. He paraded down the streets of Rome, and people flocked to watch his triumphal procession. As they chanted while he passed, his soldiers lined the streets to protect him from their outstretched arms. During the parade, a little boy, the emperor's son, jumped off the royal platform and began running between all the people. Then he darted between a guard's legs and sped toward his father. The soldier grabbed him by the neck and exclaimed: "Boy, you can't go up there!" Don't you know who that is? That's the emperor!"

The boy turned around and replied, "Mister, he may be your emperor, but he's my dad."

That's how Jesus teaches us to pray. People may have been taught that God is so distant and terrifying that we can't approach him, but he is our Father.

Praying to the Almighty

But to this Father, we say, "Hallowed be your name." God is a Father, but he's a Father in heaven whose name is hallowed. We need to remember Isaiah's lofty vision of the Lord, attended by angels with six wings who are crying out, "Holy, holy, holy is the Lord God Almighty." We should also recall Ezekiel's vision of the wheel within the middle of the wheel, and Moses' need to wear a veil because he'd seen the glory of God. He is a holy, mighty, sovereign God.

"Hallowed" means that his name is set apart. He's right here with us, and yet isn't just a big cosmic buddy. He is the holy Lord who seeks, yes even demands, our sole allegiance.

True prayer recognizes both God's loving nearness and his fearsome distance. This God will carry out his will in our world, and nothing and no one can deter him.

Praying to the King

We then pray "your kingdom come, your will be done on earth as it is in heaven." This goes way beyond praying for the church to be established. This is a blank check offered to God!

Matthew 6:10 is an example of what Old Testament scholars tell us is "synonymous parallelism." It's a common form of speech in the Old Testament where a writer would say one thing and then repeat the point through similar words.

So we pray "your kingdom come." But to reinforce that, we add "your will be done on earth as it is in heaven." We pray, in other words, for the reign of God in the whole world. We pray for everything and everyone to yield in submission to him. And, by implication, we are praying for that kingdom rule to begin in our hearts. That's why it's a blank check.

We don't just offer this prayer by easy rote. We have to be ready for God's Spirit to change us in ways we may not be ready for. We are asking God to come more powerfully, to indwell our lives, and to overtake us more than ever. So it's a prayer of submission and of repentance.

As we pray, "Your will be done on earth as it is in heaven," we're reporting for duty.

Praying to Our Provider

In addition to revealing God as our Father, as the Almighty One, and as the King, Jesus teaches us to pray remembering that he is our provider. We pray for daily bread. We seek forgiveness. We ask for deliverance from the evil one.

Some early commentators thought it was too mundane to pray for daily bread, so they spiritualized the request. They said that Jesus must surely be talking about spiritual food—since he, himself, was the Bread of Life. But he's surely talking about real food here. We turn to him declaring our utter dependence on him for life, even to the level of our daily calories.

Each of these requests stems from a humble admission that we are frail humans who are in desperate need of his care. Nothing we can do can give us the fresh start of forgiveness. That's a radical act of God. And we're so vulnerable to the evil one. Only our Father, our provider, can deliver us.

Playing for One

I've urged in this chapter that the main point isn't literal secrecy. And yet, in a culture with dozens of e-mails waiting every morning, with cell phones ringing in theaters and (let me draw a deep breath to relax before saying it) in church assemblies, with answering machines, Palm Pilots, and fax machines, it would not hurt us to take the words of Jesus literally.

The discipline of secrecy might be a way for us to get beyond all the noise and static and hear again the voice of one calling to us. There, in private, we can remember again the joy of following Jesus Christ. We can reflect on all the gifts he's showered on us. We can respond to his call of discipleship all over.

We can remind ourselves that we aren't in this life to win the approval of our parents, our neighbors, or our church. We are playing to an audience of one.

Chapter 10

THE FORGIVING CIRCLE

For if you forgive others when they sin against you, your heavenly Father will also forgive you. But if you do not forgive others their sins, your Father will not forgive your sins.
—Matthew 6:14

There is a miraculous process of forgiveness in the realm of God's rule. It begins with his forgiving act—an act which causes us to be forgiving with others. Paul captures this movement when he says that we are to "be kind and compassionate to one another, forgiving each other, just as in Christ God forgave you" (Eph. 4:32).

The miraculous process of forgiveness is captured in this wonderful parable by Lewis Smedes:

In the village of Faken in innermost Friesland there lived a long thin baker named Fouke, a righteous man, with a long thin chin and a long thin nose. Fouke was so upright that he seemed to spray righteousness from his thin lips over everyone who came near him; so the people of Faken preferred to stay away.

Fouke's wife, Hilda, was short and round, her arms were round, her bosom was round, her rump was round.

Hilda did not keep people at bay with righteousness; her soft roundness seemed to invite them instead to come close to her in order to share the warm cheer of her open heart.

Hilda respected her righteous husband, and loved him too, as much as he allowed her; but her heart ached for something more from him than his worthy righteousness.

And there, in the bed of her need, lay the seed of sadness.

One morning, having worked since dawn to knead his dough for the ovens, Fouke came home and found a stranger in his bedroom lying on Hilda's round bosom.

Hilda's adultery soon became the talk of the tavern and the scandal of the Faken congregation. Everyone assumed that Fouke would cast Hilda out of his house, so righteous was he. But he surprised everyone by keeping Hilda as his wife, saying he forgave her as the Good Book said he should.

In his heart of hearts, however, Fouke could not forgive Hilda for bringing shame to his name. Whenever he thought about her, his feelings toward her were angry and hard; he despised her as if she were a common whore. When it came right down to it, he hated her for betraying him after he had been so good and so faithful a husband to her.

He only pretended to forgive Hilda so that he could punish her with his righteous mercy.

But Fouke's fakery did not sit well in heaven.

So each time that Fouke would feel his secret hate toward Hilda, an angel came to him and dropped a small pebble, hardly the size of a shirt button, into Fouke's heart. Each time a pebble dropped, Fouke would feel a stab of pain like the pain he felt the

118

moment he came on Hilda feeding her hungry heart from a stranger's larder.

Thus he hated her the more; his hate brought him pain and his pain made him hate.

The pebbles multiplied. And Fouke's heart grew very heavy with the weight of them, so heavy that the top half of his body bent forward so far that he had to strain his neck upward in order to see straight ahead. Weary with hurt, Fouke began to wish he were dead.

The angel who dropped the pebbles into his heart came to Fouke one night and told him how he could be healed of his hurt.

There was one remedy, he said, only one, for the hurt of a wounded heart. Fouke would need the miracle of the magic eyes. He would need eyes that could look back to the beginning of his hurt and see his Hilda, not as his wife who betrayed him, but as a weak woman who needed him. Only a new way of looking at things through the magic eyes could heal the hurt flowing from the wounds of yesterday.

Fouke protested. "Nothing can change the past," he said. "Hilda is guilty, a fact that not even an angel can change."

"Yes, poor hurting man, you are right," the angel said. "You cannot change the past, you can only heal the hurt that comes to you from the past. And you can heal it only with the vision of the magic eyes."

"And how can I get your magic eyes?" pouted Fouke.

"Only ask, desiring as you ask, and they will be given you. And each time you see Hilda through your new eyes, one pebble will be lifted from your aching heart."

Fouke could not ask at once, for he had grown to love his hatred. But the pain of his heart finally drove him to want and to ask for the magic eyes that the angel had *promised. So he asked. And the angel gave.*

Soon Hilda began to change in front of Fouke's eyes, wonderfully and mysteriously. He began to see her as a needy woman who loved him instead of a wicked woman who betrayed him.

The angel kept his promise; he lifted the pebbles from Fouke's heart, one by one, though it took a long time to take them all away. Fouke gradually felt his heart grow lighter; he began to walk straight again and somehow his nose and his chin seemed less thin and sharp than before. He invited Hilda to come into his heart again, and she came, and together they began again a journey into their second season of humble joy.[1]

Our test for this chapter demands from us one of the toughest possible missions: to forgive people who hurt us, people who cause us pain. You may have some past hurt running through your mind again and again. It may feel as if it were just yesterday when that person stepped on you, and it's like the weight of an elephant pounding on your chest. It's a tough thing to do, but I pray that by the grace of God, you might begin the miraculous process of forgiving before you finish reading this chapter.

Simon Wiesenthal tells a story from World War II when he was a prisoner in a German concentration camp. As a young Jew, he was cleaning an old barn that the German soldiers had turned into a makeshift hospital. One morning a nurse came down and guided him up to the top floor where there was an SS soldier ready to die. She explained that this soldier had called for a Jew, any Jew, so that he might confess his sins against the Jewish people and might have his sins forgiven.

Wiesenthal went up there. The man clutched his hands and began recounting the time that he and his battalion of soldiers herded many Jews into a two-story house, threw gasoline on the house and lit it, and then took pot shots at anyone who dared to come out. The man said to Wiensenthal, "Behind the window of the second floor, I saw a man with a small child in his arms. His clothing was alight. By his side stood a woman, doubtless the mother of the child. With his free hand the man covered the child's eyes. Then he jumped into the street. Seconds later the mother followed. We shot . . . Oh, God . . . . I shall never forget it! It haunts me."

Then the soldier begged for Wiesenthal's forgiveness. The young Jew thought about it for a moment and then pulled his hand away, jerked around, and stormed out of the room. He recorded that in 1976 in *The Sunflower* and ended with this haunting question: "What would you have done?"[2]

Thirty-two prominent people answered Wiesenthal's question, mostly Jews, and nearly all of them said, "You did the right thing! How can you absolve someone like that? A monster! You cannot forgive people like that kind. History is doomed to repeat itself. The cycle goes on and on if we forgive people of those kinds of hurts!" Nothing brings down the silly, pat answers liked rugged reality.

Consider the woman I know who had been married for a nearly two decades. Together she and her husband had three children, raised mostly by her. She had been there when he was trying to make ends meet. When it was necessary, she had taken a job on the side just so they could pay the bills. He tried climbing the corporate ladder and had to attend business-related parties. She had endured the parties to play the part of the supportive wife, and she had always been there when he was depressed, when his self-esteem was low. Finally he started to make it in the corporate world. Then one day he broke the news: he'd met someone else, someone younger, someone who understood him and who really supported him, and he was leaving. Would you forgive if you were his wife?

How about a good friend of mine who, fresh out of graduate training, became a minister for a church in the Southeast? His love and enthusiasm were infectious. These were joyful times for the little congregation.

But there was one church leader, probably motivated by jealousy, who thought it was his task in life to ruin my friend. He made life miserable for him, trying to convince others that he wasn't a reliable minister. Finally, the leader railroaded my friend out of town. Would you forgive?

Or consider the mother who has to skip several suppers with her family because the husband gambles or drinks away all the money. What of the many people I've met who were molested by morally bent parents or step-parents?

There's an even larger number who didn't have morally bent parents, but morally straight parents who could never love them. At church the parents were saints, but at home they were standoffish, antiseptic, and judgmental. So they never loved their kids, never rocked them, never held them close and told them they were special. Their friends were never good enough. They could never do enough to satisfy the parents. How do you forgive?

Maybe you were denied a promotion because someone you thought was close to you denied you a good word at the needed moment. Maybe you're still feeling the pain of parents who doted on your little brother or sister while they treated you as if you were an accident, an unwelcome one at that. Perhaps you're a daughter whose drunken father always embarrassed you when you brought a boyfriend home. How do you forgive?

How about that drunken teenager who killed someone's son? In just six months he's out on parole. He's slapped on the wrist, and before yo know it he's had three more drunk driving charges. He's free. The son's in the grave.

What about the invisible people? How do you forgive the parent whom you resented all these years and who is now dead? The child who committed suicide and has cause all this bitterness on your part? The mother who gave you away when you were a baby and has made you think all these years that you were not worth keeping? The monster who haunts a friend of mine in Tennessee every night after taking one evening of her life?

I don't give all these examples for emotional effect. I give them because we are real people, and injustice stings us, just like it does anyone else. When we've been blistered by injustice, the easiest response is to stew in hatred. There's something infectious about hate, something energizing. But there's something stronger than hate that will last when hate won't. It's forgiveness.

What is this forgiveness? When Jesus said, "If you forgive others when they sin, your heavenly Father will also forgive you," what did he mean? Let's begin through the back door with what forgiveness is *not*.

What Forgiveness is Not

Forgiving is not forgetting. Some of you have mentally flogged yourself because you forgave somebody but keep remembering the hurt. How in the world did you think you could forget it? You're not a computer. It's not as though you can bring it up in a Word document and punch the delete key. The memory cells are there. We cannot exorcize them. The real test of forgiving is the healing of that lingering pain so that you view people in a different way as the pain begins to be removed. You see them with a new vision.

Someone might ask, "Well, doesn't God forgive and forget?" Yes and no. God said at the end of Isaiah 43, "I, even I, am he who blots our your transgressions, ... and remembers your sins no more" (v. 25). But that doesn't mean our sin is blotted out of his mind as if he didn't know it ever existed. It means God puts sin behind him. He treats us as he would have treated us had we never sinned. He acts toward us as he would have acted had we never turned our backs on him. Does Jesus know who betrayed him? If you asked him today, would he know the name of the man? Yes. Does that remove his words, "Father, forgive them"? No.

Forgiving *does* involve forgetting to the extent that we put it behind us. We don't dwell on it. So many times in our family relationships, especially, we just torture ourselves to death by constantly bringing out the past offense every time there's an argument. One man went to a counselor and said, "Every time we fight, my wife gets historical!"

The counselor said, "You mean hysterical."

He said, "No, historical. She brings everything up from the past."

Forgiving will involve putting things behind us. But it's not forgetting.

Forgiving is also not repressing conflict. As parents, we want our children to be so good that we tell them, "Now, don't get mad. Don't be angry with your brother or sister. Forget that he did that. Forget that she wrote all over your wall or destroyed your picture. You just forget all that." We're setting the stage for some kids to be driven crazy by repressed anger.

There's conflict that needs to be brought to the surface in some churches, in families, and in offices, because if it's not up at the surface, it will be festering right *under* the surface. It will be on slow boil, and someday it will explode. So forgiveness is not suppressing conflict.

Third, forgiveness is not tolerating evil. Suppose a drunk driver killed somebody close to you and you find it in your heart finally to forgive. The pebbles are slowly removed from your heart and you get those magic eyes. Should you still prosecute? Yes, because forgiving is not tolerating. Where would our society be if we became so milquetoast in our toleration that we did not allow rehabilitation and rebuking? Sometimes we forgive but still follow through with tough love.

Four Steps in Forgiveness

What is forgiveness? Lewis Smedes identifies four steps of forgiveness. The first step is hurting. Somebody hurt you. Now, this is not talking about some small offense that is so insignificant you ought to just shrug it off and go on. There are some things about which we ought to say, "Well, you know, I have days like that," and just roll with the punches.

When somebody steps on you and really hurts you, however, it will be personal. I don't have to forgive Joseph Stalin.

Real hurt isn't just personal; it's also deep. It's not some superficial wound where we can just roll with the punches, but something deep—someone has stepped on us, somebody has betrayed us, somebody has violated us, someone has let us down. That's the first stage, real hurting. You've been there, haven't you?

That leads to the second stage, where the hurting turns into hating. This isn't just a momentary anger, but a real hating. You have this aggressive desire to persecute somebody, or at least a passive desire for something not to go well with the person. Both are hate; they're just different kinds.

The third stage is healing—the new eyes of Smedes' parable. It comes when I start to look at somebody with new vision, with new possibility. I'm looking more toward the future than the past. The healing process does not deny the hurt or the hating, but it says, "I will quit that. I'm going to release the other person from my animosity. Whether she wants that or not, I'm going to go on."

Finally there's the fourth stage, the coming together in reconciliation. We're responsible only for the first three stages. All we can do is start the healing process by bringing the bitterness up from the dark recesses of our hearts and releasing it. But there's no guarantee of reconciliation, because some people will reject all attempts at reconciliation. That's the goal, however—to go to the person, to be reconciled.

Why Should We Forgive?

Why should we forgive? You may have suffered pain for a long time. Perhaps there are some people you've hated for all too long. Why should you forgive them?

The main reason is very clear in Matthew 6. It's because that's the way of God. God forgives us. Jesus teaches us to pray, "Forgive us our debts, as we also have forgiven our debtors." Then he notes, "For if you forgive others when they sin against you, your heavenly Father will also forgive you."

We need to be careful in reading those passages. The Lord's Prayer is a disciple's prayer. It's for people who are already in relationship with God. Jesus wasn't saying that if we're forgiving people, the blood of Christ will then wash away our sins. We're saved by God's grace channeled through our faith. Salvation is a gift of God as his kingdom breaks through. But as disciples, we understand that when we stand in the icy hell of unforgiveness, we're standing in rebellion against God. We're not walking in the light. We haven't even understood our forgiveness.

If you cross the bridge of forgiveness and then light a fire to it, you have burned your own path to forgiveness. An old tradition has General Oglethorpe saying to John Wesley, "I never forgive and I never forget."

To which Wesley was supposed to have responded, "Then, dear sir, I hope you never sin."

Jesus said it's a cycle. God initiated it. He forgave us. And now, as disciples, we're to walk in the light and keep the forgiveness going. Somebody's got to break that merry-go-round of hate.

Our ability to forgive others begins in the realization that there is darkness within us as well. We have contributed to the brokenness of this world. We have our own capacity for evil and our own need for God's costly grace. Without this understanding, our quest to forgive others will be condescending and trite, perhaps even filled with victimizing language.

Christianity holds this foundational truth: You forgive not primarily because it will heal you but because you have received forgiveness from God. You forgive others because "in Christ God forgave you."

While we don't forgive for our own benefit, it is nevertheless true that we are much healthier as a result.

Our own sanity demands it. If we start waiting for that last pound of flesh, we're in trouble. We're the ones who pay for it. That monster out there who took that one night from the life of a girl in Tennessee will get just what he wants, which is to destroy her, if she refuses to forgive, if she refuses to begin the healing process.

Lewis Smedes wrote this in *Christianity Today*:

> *To forgive is to put down your fifty-pound pack after a ten-mile climb of a mountain. To forgive is to fall into a chair after a fifteen-mile marathon. To forgive is to set a prisoner free and discover that the prisoner was you. To forgive is to reach back into your hurting past and recreate it in your memory so that you can begin again. To forgive is to dance to the beat of God's forgiving heart. It's to ride the crest of love's strongest wave. Our only escape from history's cruel unfairness, our only passage to the future's creative possibilities, is the miracle of forgiving.*

For our own good, our own spiritual sanity, we have to let the hatred go.

Finally, we forgive because relationships are worth it. The ones we withhold forgiveness from are usually the ones closest to us. Why do we love to destroy our marriages? Why do we love to hate our kids or our parents or the people who live next to us? Why do we love to hate those relationships? Relationships are all we have! As Ghandi said, if we live by the "eye for eye" mentality, eventually everybody's blind. That's truer in close relationships than anywhere else.

In one of his writings, my good friend Rubel Shelly relates a true and moving story of a woman who walked down the church aisle, bearing a confession of marital infidelity. With tears running down her cheeks she handed the minister a prepared statement in which she confessed her sin and asked for the forgiveness and support of the church.

As her statement was being read, somebody got up from the audience, walked down to the front, and put his arm around her. It was her husband.

The Goal: Reconciliation

In Matthew 18, Jesus talked about the value of each human being. The disciples asked the question, "Who is the greatest in the kingdom of heaven?" Their question betrayed the way they were overlooking the value of any individual who did not contribute to their ongoing climbing of the kingdom ladder. Jesus responded by pointing out a little child and saying, "This is the kingdom. This is the business of God's reign in the world. It's this child." We are about the major business of the kingdom when we reach out even to a little child, because everyone is of worth in God's kingdom.

Next Jesus called for reconciliation: "If a brother or sister sins, go and point out the fault, just between the two of you alone. If they listen to you, you have won them over" (Matt. 18:15).

Relationships matter so much that we need to get beyond our conflict avoidance and initiate reconciliation. Jesus goes so far as to describe the next steps for reconciliation when a face-to-face meeting doesn't work. God's view of this is clear: where two or more are gathered in his name (presumably, in this context, to work out problems), God is right there.

Peter asked the question, "Lord, how many times shall I forgive someone who sins against me? Up to seven times?" He thought that was supermagnanimous. Nobody would be that bold!

But Jesus replied, "I tell you, not seven times, but seventy-seven times" (Matt. 18:22). Just keep on forgiving. Keep that circle of forgiveness rolling.

The Unmerciful Servant

With all that as background in Matthew 18, we come to the parable of the unmerciful servant. We are all in the position of this servant to one extent or another. The story begins in verse 23, and the first lesson we learn from it is that God's servant receives God's forgiveness. It tells of a servant who owed his master a huge debt, one he could never repay. But the master was gracious, and took pity, canceling the debt and letting him go.

After being forgiven his enormous debt, however, the unmerciful servant turned right around and had a fellow servant who owed him a pittance thrown into debtors' prison. By refusing to extend the same mercy he had been shown, the servant burned the bridge he had walked over. So the master said, "All right. You want to play by the rules of merit. Great! We'll all play by the rules of merit. If everybody has to come to you with a pound of flesh, then you come to me with a pound of flesh." You stand in rebellion against God if you cannot extend compassion as he has extended it to you.

On the cross Jesus took pity on people who had been chanting for his death and gambling for his clothes. What were his words? "Father, forgive them. They don't have any idea what they're doing." He didn't remove the responsibility they bore, but he had compassion and cut the cord of hatred.

You don't know the full story of your enemies. You don't know everything that went on with those parents who made living so tough for you. You don't know all the circumstances of that person at church who lashed out in anger that day. They're still responsible for the hurt they caused. Nothing excuses somebody from stepping on you. But once you see them with the magic eyes of forgiveness, you can start to let the pebbles be taken from our hearts.

The process of forgiveness is often very slow.

C. S. Lewis told about a monster he had for a teacher when he was a boy. It seemed this academic sadist always had it in for him and the others in his class. And Lewis felt he could never forgive him. But just before the end of his life, Lewis wrote to an American friend: "Do you know, only a few weeks ago, I realized suddenly that I had at last forgiven the cruel schoolmaster who so darkened my childhood. I'd been trying to do it for years."

That's the spirit God is looking for. It's not as though all of a sudden—poof!—everything is forgiven. But it's amazing how, slowly pebble by pebble, God starts to reframe us. Our thinking is a little different, and the rerun of hatred ceases to show in our minds.

Corrie Ten Boom, who went through all kinds of terrible experiences in a German concentration camp in World War II, often said the thing she remembered most was being in the shower with the other women to have all the lice washed away. She especially remembered the lecherous eyes of the German guards as they stood and watched.

But finally she got to the point that she thought she had forgiven the guards by the grace of God, and she was happy. It felt like a freedom to forgive even those people who had taken away something that was closer to her than even her heart. When the war was over, she went around the world preaching about forgiveness.

One day she went to Munich, where she spoke on the beauty of God's love. When she was done, a man walked up and said, "Yes, Fraulein, it's wonderful that Jesus forgives us all our sins, just as you say." He had his hand stuck out to shake hers, but she recognized the face. She could identify the lecherous eyes of a guard who had stood there peering at her. Now he was saying he was thankful for the forgiveness she'd just spoken about, and he wanted to shake her hand. Her hand, however, was frozen to her side. She thought she had forgiven, but in her heart of hearts she had not. Realizing that, she broke down before God and prayed that he would forgive her for that lack of compassion. And as she began to feel forgiven, she then could be forgiving to the guard. So she extended her hand and said, "Yes, it is."

Doesn't some healing need to take place in your life?

Isn't it time to cut loose the wrongs of the past and to sail freely into the future? God Almighty will help you. This is, indeed, righteousness that surpasses the Pharisees and the teachers of the law—a righteousness that comes from a forgiven heart.

Chapter 11
WHERE IS YOUR
TREASURE BURIED?

Do not store up for yourselves treasures on earth, where
moth and rust destroy, and where thieves break in and steal.
—Matthew 6:19

The old cigar box gives you no clue what treasures are contained within. But this worn out box, still in my possession, holds some of my boyhood wealth.

There is my KODE-TV channel 12 Ranger Ed membership badge. My cousin and I were fanatics. We were entertainment-challenged, growing up before Sesame Street, Mr. Rogers, Lambchops, Barney, or Blues Clues. But we had Ranger Ed. Once Ranger Ed had a contest, saying he'd give away a horse to the boy or girl in the four-state area (Missouri, Kansas, Oklahoma, and Arkansas) who sent in the best name for the horse. My cousin won, suggesting the name "Ride-a-Lot." I never won a horse, of course, but I had a badge. I was an OFFICIAL member of the Ranger Ed club.

The cigar box also has my Smokey the Bear membership badge and bookmarker, some old tickets to a Cub Scout Jamboree, old soda bottle caps with football players underneath, a postcard of Lassie (all right, we weren't completely deprived of entertainment), and a treasure map from Biloxi, which I was sure did indeed lead to buried loot.

My mom saved this box for me through all those years when I'd outgrown my treasures. This is ironic, because this is the same woman who threw away all my baseball cards from the 1960s—cards that would now be worth thousands of dollars (especially since I was always a Mickey Mantle and Willie Mays fan). She pitched the cards and kept the cardboard box.

But I'm glad to have my old cigar box of goodies. For as a boy, these were my gems. I wouldn't have traded them for anything.

I guess most people have had a box like that—even people in concentration camps or jail. Last year I spent a weekend with the teenagers from our church ministering to and being ministered to by homeless people in our city. The leaders of our "life on the streets" experience had us walk several miles down a railroad track to the edge of town, then led us through some trees to a hidden homeless camp. The individuals who lived there welcomed us and showed us their lean-to "homes." Every single one of them had something like my cigar box—something that contained their deepest treasures: an old military medal, a faded photo of a former love, or a well-worn Bible.

A couple of weeks ago, I took all my 8-mm home tapes to a business that would convert them to DVD. As I handed them over, I found myself choking back tears. "Sir," I said, "I'm sorry. But my daughter died a few years ago and these are all the tapes I have of her. I can't stand the thought of something happening to them. It's hard to hand them over." The older man nodded knowingly and said, "I understand. My daughter died too. I won't lose your tapes."

Because the reign of God has broken in, Jesus tells us to evaluate our box of treasures. What is it we really value?

His words cut right to the heart of life in the Western world. If idolatry is trying to find life in something (or someone) other than God, we are an idol-filled civilization. So much of life consists of consuming and expanding.

We've come to expect luxury—in our homes (with average square footage rising constantly), in our vehicles, and in our vacations. It has never been as true as it is today that the poor are getting poorer while the wealthy are getting wealthier—even while complaining that they don't have enough.

The School of Insatiability

In my university classes on "The Life and Teachings of Jesus," I've often asked my students, "What is your favorite story in the gospels about Jesus?" Nearly every possible story has been named.

One that has not yet been nominated is the encounter of Jesus with the "rich young ruler." It's a story we'd just as soon pass on. This eager young Command-Keeper was stung by these words: "One thing you lack. Go, sell everything you have and give to the poor, and you will have treasure in heaven. Then come, follow me" (Mark 10:21).

Now there's a kick in the gut! What this young man heard was, "Forget it, Pal. You have a fat chance of getting eternal life." His face fell, and he snuck away sad.

But there is one crucial little detail mentioned only by Mark. Before telling us what Jesus said, Mark informs us that "Jesus looked at him and loved him." The whole story hangs on this little piece of info.

Jesus wasn't scolding; he certainly wasn't bludgeoning. He was looking deeply into this man like a physician who's trying to make a diagnosis of an illness. It was the same look he gave a blind man who needed sight or a bleeding woman who needed healing.

Because he loved this young man, he told him something no one else would likely tell him.

That still holds true today. If you struggle with overeating, society will offer its help. If you battle drug or alcohol addictions, then friends, physicians, therapists, or recovery group members will jump to your aid.

But what about someone who is in love with money, with consumption, with shopping, with retirement accounts, with possessions? Don't hold your breath waiting for a campaign that warns you about lust for stuff!

Our economy is largely build on consumption and over-consumption. As Rodney Clapp has insightfully written, "The affluent, technologically advanced West seems more and more focused not on consuming to live but on living to consume." Advertisers want you to believe that your life is missing something—until you rent their vacation house, until you purchase their SUV, until you dine at their luxury restaurant, until you have the newest technology.

Regis's "Who Wants to Be a Millionaire?" did so well for a couple of years (until we got overexposed!) because there's an implicit assumption: everyone would! Don't hold your breath for a follow-up show called "Who Wants to Be a Peace Corps Worker?" It just wouldn't fly!

There was, however, a program that followed called "Who Wants to Marry a Millionaire?" And then Fox followed suit with "Joe Millionaire"—a show that tricked some young women into thinking that the eligible bachelor was a multi-millionaire, when in truth he was a blue-collar worker making under twenty grand a year. Viewers expressed their shock at the blatant gold digging of the women. (Apparently not as many were bothered by the blatant lies of the network in telling them he was someone he wasn't.)

We have all been educated in the school of insatiability. We need just a little more. To consume is to enjoy, and to enjoy is to live. Life is found in the abundance of things. So as a result, families across the board are saving less and borrowing more. Nearly everyone, whether their home has 800 square feet or 8000 square feet, thinks they need just a little more. Nearly everyone, whether their income is $15,000 or $150,000 thinks they could be happy if they made just 20% more. The real issue isn't income. It's insatiability.

Jesus' words came like a stun gun because he loved this man. He wanted to tell him the truth that no one else would tell him. He wanted him to know that life is NOT found in the abundance of stuff. He wanted to warn him about the funny things insatiability and dissatisfaction can do to your life. He wanted to raise red flags about the bizarre ways we tie net worth and income to self-worth and power.

Material Treasures Aren't to be Stored

So we need to ask ourselves where our treasures are buried. What's in the "old cigar box" of our hearts?

What Jesus is forbidding is the selfish accumulation of goods that runs rampant around us. Notice he said, "Don't store up for yourselves." It's not the presence of resources for the service of Christ, but building up treasuries for ourselves, the kind of extravagant living that believes in the fantasy that life consists in having an abundance of things: the more you get, the better off you are. If you could just have a little better house or a little better car, you could have it made. Life would be abundant. You would be rich. That's the philosophy he was talking about.

Then the master Teacher explains why: "For where your treasure is, there your heart will be also." If God came down and said, "Let me find your heart," where would He find it? Is it in a bank account? Is it in a college degree?

The reason you can look at a man's or woman's treasure and find that person's heart is that it was the heart that made it a treasure in the first place. Picture a pile of hay and a pile of gold. Neither is intrinsically of greater value. If I were on an island about to die of cold, I would rather have a pile of hay—if I had a match. It's a question of what you put your heart into.

A biographer of the Duke of Wellington said that an old account ledger showing how the duke had spent his money was a far better clue to what he thought was really important than his letters or speeches. That's just what Jesus says. If you want to find a person's heart, start flipping through his checkbook.

Material Things Can't Be Stored

A second principle comes right on the heels of the first: Material possessions *cannot* be stored up. Jesus' explanation is that earthly wealth is kept "where moth and rust destroy, and where thieves break in and steal." Everything goes! Moths may eat it; rust may corrode it; thieves may steal it. You can't hold on to things on this earth.

That possession you killed yourself for two years ago

is probably stuck up in the attic right now. The clothes you just had to have are out of style. You just can't keep things. Three years ago the Associated Press ran an article about how that was literally true. It said a cotton farmer in another country had buried $150 for safe-keeping. It was to be used for his wedding. But the wedding had to be called off, because he had buried it near a colony of ants, and they ate his bank notes. So he went crying out to the authorities, "Look! The ants ate my money!" They said, "You should have kept your money in the bank where it would have been safe."

Let me tell you something about banks, however. They're not safe, either, from Jesus' perspective. My older son, now a university student, still remembers when someone broke into our house and stole his bank—all right, admittedly a little piggy bank. But still, it was a major heist to him. For years after that, whenever we couldn't find something around the house he said, "Someone probably stole it!"

We think we're a little more sophisticated than the people in Jesus' day, because we pride ourselves on protection. Moths don't harm us much because we have mothballs and insecticides. To combat rust we have rust-proof paint. For thieves we have the FDIC, burglar alarms, fences, homeowner's policies, neighborhood watch groups, and big dogs. We look out for thieves.

We put our money in municipal bonds, precious metals, commodities, savings bonds, CD's, mutual funds, money market accounts, real estate, and a hundred other investments. But the pertinent question is, Are these investments our treasure—or is the kingdom our true treasure with these as resources for service in the kingdom?

The words of Jesus still apply. We cannot lay up for

ourselves treasures on earth. It may not be moths, rust, or thieves that destroy it. But something will get it. If nothing else, eternity will get it.

A scene I'll never forget following the terrorist attacks of September 11, 2001, was Diane Sawyer standing in soot near where the World Trade Center had stood just hours before. She picked up some random papers off the street and said, "Yesterday, all these papers probably meant everything to someone. These are papers about investments and deals. But today they mean nothing."

Heavenly Treasures Can Be Stored

In contrast, eternal treasures, or heavenly investments, can be stored up. "Store up for yourselves treasures in heaven," Jesus challenges us, "where moth and rust do not destroy, and where thieves do not break in and steal" (Matt. 6:20). Those treasures are protected. Even death can't touch them. A heavenly investment is always a bullish investment. Thieves, moths, rust, economic downturns, oil shortages—you name it—nothing can take away a heavenly investment.

Jesus illustrates his point:

> The eye is the lamp of the body. If your eyes are healthy, your whole body will be full of light. But if your eyes are unhealthy, your whole body will be full of darkness. If then the light within you is darkness, how great is that darkness!
>
> Matt. 6:22f

The eye here represents your heart, your mind, your perspective, what you value. It's what you let into your life. If your eyes let in light—that is, if they're set on heavenly treasures—your whole life is filled with light. If your eyes are closed, though, closed to these heavenly treasures, then the body is eaten through with corruption. There's just darkness to be found there. Even the light within you is darkness, he says paradoxically.

The county can evaluate my property, but the county cannot evaluate my treasures. I'd love for the country assessor to come knocking on my door some Monday morning, saying, "I'd like to see your treasures."

I'd say, "You mean my property."

Maybe he would say, "No, I want to see your treasures."

I would love it. He'd be in for an earful about what is most important in life in view of the in-breaking of God's rule. When you invest in the kingdom of God, you're investing in something that lasts.

Challenges for Today

A couple of challenges grow out of Jesus' teaching. One is to re-examine our emphasis on stuff. I once preached a few sermons on materialism. I'll never forget those who responded to me as if I had overreacted. Their attitude was "poor little preacher. He gets so worked up about these things." Their attitude was, "We don't struggle with materialism. We don't place our trust in things. We like to have them, and we like to have them in abundance. But we don't make them our treasures."

How would we respond to the story Jesus told about the fool who kept building bigger and bigger barns for his wealth? Jesus warned: "Watch out! Be on your guard against all kinds of greed; life does not consist in an abundance of possessions" (Luke 12:15). Or what if we'd heard him say, "Children, how hard it is to enter the kingdom of God! It is easier for a camel to go through the eye of a needle than for the rich to enter the kingdom of God" (Mark 10:24f).

Would we dismissively say to each other, "You know, that was great, but that doesn't apply to us. I mean, that stuff about a camel and the eye of a needle! We don't struggle with that. That applies to somebody else."

Well, to whom does it apply? Wasn't he talking to people who claimed to follow in the footsteps of God? I think materialism is *the* struggle of God's church today. Beneath our materialistic behavior lies a value system and even a worldview that are idolatrous. We too often do believe that life is found in the abundance of possessions.

The problem with the rich fool wasn't that he took his crops and stored them. That sounds like good farming to me. The problem with the rich fool was that he took his crops and put them in his heart. We need Christ-followers who can handle wealth with simplicity and generosity.

A second challenge is to reorient our lives toward the imperishable God. The teacher in a third-grade Bible school class was talking about marriage and the sanctity of marriage, and she decided to talk for just a moment about bigamy. So she asked the class, "Can anybody quote a verse of Scripture that shows it's wrong for a man to have two wives?" A little boy raised his hand and came up with Matthew 6:24: "No one can serve two masters."

You cannot serve two masters. This is more practical reality than uncommon insight: "Either you're going to love one and hate the other or you're going to love that one and despise the first." Dietrich Bonhoeffer expressed the thought well: "Our hearts have room only for one all-embracing devotion, and we can only cleave to one Lord." Only one person can be telling you what to do if you're a slave.

God and Money

Finally, Jesus said, "You cannot serve God and Money" (v. 24). Some people think you can. Their philosophy is, "I will serve God on Sundays. Weekdays will be spent for money." Jesus says, "Uh uh. That won't do. If that's your philosophy, you're only serving one god—money." Some think, "I will invest my lips with God and my life with money." But that won't work either. You can serve only one master. God doesn't want to share the throne of your life with anyone or anything, whether with you or a spouse or money.

The Pharisees tried to straddle the fence. Note that Jesus doesn't say no one can *try* to serve two masters, because they were trying it. But Jesus said we cannot in actual living love both God and money; it just won't work.

If you want righteousness that flows from the heart, you must come to a fundamental decision. What do I want to be? Or more fundamentally in this text, whose do I want to be? Who will be the master? What is my ambition for life? Is it possible that spiritual frustrations and failures come because we're trying to serve two masters?

Sigmund Freud had a favorite story about a sailor who was shipwrecked on one of the South Sea islands. When he woke up, he had been hoisted to the shoulders of some natives, and they were carrying him to a crude throne. And on this makeshift, crude throne, he started asking what was happening. They said, "You are king of this island for a year." He liked that idea. He could have anything he wanted. But then he got to thinking, "Where are the earlier kings?"

He learned that at the end of his year, so there wouldn't be competition between kings, he was to be stranded on a deserted island to starve to death. You can imagine that took a little of the fun out of it. But he began immediately to plan his strategy. He discovered which island was to be his. Then he had his carpenters build boats. Next he had his farmers get on the boats and take fruit trees over to that island and plant them and other crops. Then he got the masons and carpenters together, and they went over on the boats and built places for him to be shaded. Finally he sent provisions over and people who could make clothing. By the end of his year as king, he had a nice, well-equipped island where a person could live forever.

Where are our investments going? All of us can be king of something, but are we putting our efforts into things that will last or living just for today? If our treasures are invested in loving God and in loving others, our investments are secure. That's an island that will never be deserted. But if we're spending our lives on bigger barns, more crops, and more money, we're in for a tragic loss.

Satan takes his lasso of materialism, puts it over the neck of the church, and tightens it as far as we'll let him. He'll let us be as orthodox as we want to be. He'll concede every belief the Bible affirms and be glad that we affirm them if we'll only believe the illusion that life is found in the abundance of things.

Baby Steps

We are so enmeshed in consumerism that we can hardly escape it completely. Most of us won't take vows of poverty. But wouldn't it be wise, in light of the constant warnings of our Lord and the pressing needs of our world, if we took small-but-constant steps of resistence?

What if we meditated more and talked in our Bible classes more about the words of Jesus that relate to wealth? What if we heard them in all their bald affront before writing them off? "Go, sell everything you have and give to the poor." "Do not store up for yourselves treasures on earth." "Woe to you who are rich, for you have already received your comfort." "Life is more than food, and the body more than clothes." "Be on your guard against all kinds of greed."

What if we learned to be thankful? Try it: the next time you are consumed by the desire to purchase something someone else has, stop and list the things you are grateful for. Here's part of my list: a woman who has loved me for nearly a quarter of a century; a college student with a heart for God; his fourth-grade brother who lets me coach his little league team; a roof over my head; a job that is meaningful; health insurance; friends who know the worst about me and love me anyway. When I stop and think about those things, the tug of insatiability begins to lessen.

What if we learned to share? Malcolm Street realized that as a wealthy Texan it was just too easy for him to ignore the needs of people all around him. So he began giving generously. He started taking mission trips to places like Haiti and Honduras. He built and then operated apartments for frail elderly people who needed assistance. And he lives well below his means so he can be near people with the greatest needs—people with whom he also leads a regular Bible study. Sure, Malcolm Street is rare. But . . . couldn't we all make sacrifices in order to share with people who need housing, food, job training, and medical care?

When my older son graduated from high school, our family took a graduation trip. We joined some mission families in Uganda for a month. Several times a week we traveled out into the villages where they were planting churches, amazed at what God was doing through their ministry.

On our first Sunday with a village church, the missionary with us told us that if we'd like to give something for the collection we were welcome to. But he said they recommend that people not give over 5,000 Ugandan shillings—or about three American dollars. He said that too much might overwhelm them, because they had no reference for our wealth. So we gave that amount. The total contribution that day, after everyone offered their gift, was the equivalent of $3.07. The rest of the church had given out of their (from our point of view) poverty an amount equal to seven pennies.

When I asked what they'd do each week with seven cents, he told us that this money had three uses: they would buy a few bricks for their building, they would help support someone to ride his bike into the next village to preach, and they would save a little for someone whose crops might not come in that year.

Amazing! We were bowled over by the wealth we take for granted. It made us eager to make sure, like our Ugandan brothers and sisters, that we know where our true treasures are buried.

Chapter 12
THE PROFESSIONAL WORRY WART

So do not worry, saying, "What shall we eat?" or
"What shall we drink?" or "What shall we wear?" For
the pagans run after all these things, and your heavenly
Father knows that you need them.
—Matthew 6:31f

"All her life she was a worrier, brooding like a hen over terrors to come almost as though to hatch them out into reality would be kind of a relief because there at least she could come to some sort of terms with them as in her dark dreams she could not."

Those are Frederick Buechner's words about his grandmother in his spiritual journey entitled *A Sacred Journey.* All her life she was a worrier. And I'll not be the first one to pick up a stone to throw at her.

My freshman year in college, my stomach began hurting regularly in a way it had never hurt before. I couldn't explain it. I tried our family miracle drug, Pepto-Bismol, but that didn't work. So I pulled out one of those medical guides that are a lot like car repair manuals. You look up the problem, and it gives all the options for what might be wrong. Under "Stomach Problems—Chronic," it listed everything from indigestion, which I didn't believe it was, to pregnancy, which I was sure it wasn't.

Then I went to visit a doctor, who told me that at the ripe age of eighteen I had an ulcer. So the words of Matthew 6 have been words I've focused on since then as I seek to temper my type A personality, control stress, and master worry.

I imagine this chapter being written to an audience of one. From me to me. My name is Mike, and I am a worrier. I worry about many things, but I have one special anxiety that at times is controlling. Since my daughter's death in 1994, I've worried about the health and safety of my sons. All parents are concerned, I'm sure. But I fret, stew, and sweat. I confess to you that I write these words as one who has seen a more trusting way—a way that fits better my belief that the kingdom has broken in—and am seeking, with the help of my friends and my covenant group, to follow.

The people to whom Jesus spoke knew worry all too well. The large majority just tried to hammer out a meager existence. They, like so many today, knew how important it was just to receive "daily bread." Most of them knew that if there wasn't enough snow in the winter in the northern mountains, there would be a drought the following summer. They knew that if there wasn't enough rain, the food supply was in trouble. If the locusts showed up in full force or if there was an invasion of the land, there might not be enough food for everybody.

But we live in a wealthy nation, relatively speaking. A Third World citizen might suppose worry has passed us by since we don't have to worry about the snows and whether we'll eat or not. That's not the case, however. We create more things to worry about. In the absence of some of the real worries of people in Jesus' day, we have manufactured our own. The words of Erma Bombeck are insightful:

> I've always worried a lot and frankly, I'm good at it. I worry about introducing people and going blank when I get to my mother. I worry about a shortage of ball bearings, a snake coming up through the kitchen drain. I worry about the world ending at midnight and getting stuck with three hours on a twenty-four hour cold capsule. I worry about getting into the Guinness Book of World Records under "Pregnancy: Oldest Recorded Birth." I worry what the dog thinks when he sees me coming out of the shower; that one of my children will marry an Eskimo who will set me adrift on an iceberg when I can no longer feed myself. I worry about salesladies following me into the fitting room, oil slicks, and Carol Channing going bald. I worry about scientists discovering someday that lettuce has been fattening all along.

What are your worries? Maybe finances are your major concern. Are you worried about how to make your next car payment? About how to get the creditors off your back? After a year of juggling bills, taking turns making different ones late, has it caught up with you? Do you wonder how to get past the near knockout punch of some hospital bill when your twenty percent after insurance is more than you make in six months? Have you no idea how to face the cost of one more (maybe unexpected!) child soon to be born or one more child about to enter college? How to stretch your Social Security check when your rent goes up? How to earn enough money when you graduate in May to pay off your student loans? How to get braces on your fourth grader, a new transmission in your Buick, a retirement home for your widowed mom?

Perhaps you worry about death, whether it will be soon or distant; whether it will come in a car, on a plane, or in an ICU ward. Maybe there's a history of cancer or heart problems in your family. You carry around those worries with you every moment of every day. Maybe you worry about whether you'll get married or not. Or perhaps you're a vicarious worrier, so you worry about whether your kids will ever get married.

One French philosopher put it this way: "My life has been full of misfortunes—most of which never happened." To a large degree, that's us—worried about things most of which will never occur. Somebody said, "Worry is interest paid on trouble before it's due." Another said, "Worry is faith in the negative, trust in the unpleasant, assurance of disaster, and belief of defeat."

Jesus' Teaching

Matthew 6:25 begins with "therefore," a key word that should have a little arrow pointing back as if to say, "Based on what I just told you about the decision you have to make regarding masters, and since I'm urging you to choose God, *therefore*, I tell you don't worry." That's the refrain that takes us through the rest of Matthew 6.

Notice, however, that he didn't say we should never be concerned or show precaution. Some people misunderstand this and think they have to be so totally laid back that they never take precaution in anything. Imagine the family sitting around the table and the wife says, "Honey, the kids have been playing on the highway again."

He replies, "That's all right. Don't worry about it. The Lord will take care of them."

It doesn't mean we go without fire alarms or leave our doors unlocked. But there's a difference between a healthy precaution and an unhealthy worry—the kind of anxiety that fills our mental hospitals. There are a couple of illustrations in the biblical text.

"Is not life more important than food, and the body more important than clothes?" (V. 25). "Look at the birds of the air; they do not sow or reap or store away in barns, and yet your heavenly Father feeds them" (v. 26). That's the life of a bird. It goes about its business. It's not nearly as energetic in a diversified way in producing food as we are. It's energetic, but not over-whelmed by sowing and reaping. It doesn't build barns to put the food into.

Does that mean the bird doesn't work for its food? No. The bird doesn't just wake up in the morning and open its mouth, waiting for the sky to rain worms. It goes out and scratches and digs, because God has programmed it to go after food. But it doesn't get all uptight about it.

There are a couple of poems I've come across that deal with the way the animal kingdom seems to be carefree.

> Said the robin to the sparrow,
> I should really like to know
> Why those anxious human beings
> Rush about and worry so.
> Said the sparrow to the robin,
> Well, I think that it must be
> That they have no heavenly Father
> Such as cares for you and me.

There's one I like even better, though:

There was a young lady from Ryde
Who was carried away by the tide
A man-eating shark
Was heard to remark
I knew the Lord would provide.

"Aren't you much more valuable than they?" Jesus asked. That's a typical rabbinic argument, going from the lesser to the greater. You make the point about the birds. Then you play your trump card: "Now look. If that's true in this little regard right here, how much more true it is over here!" If God will take care of a bird, surely he'll take care of you.

Jesus highlights the uselessness of worry: "Who of you by worrying can add a single hour to his life?" Imagine going to your cardiologist and receiving this advice: "Look, you've got some severe heart problems. You keep living the way you're living and you're going to die in two years. Now this is what I recommend. Take a month off from work and worry about it all day long."

Would a doctor ever do that? Not likely. Or imagine a church out in the country. They're worried because there's been no rain for two months. So they announce on Sunday morning, "We're going to meet for two hours this afternoon and worry about it together." Why don't they do that? We all recognize the uselessness of worry.

Worry never changes a C to an A. Worry never changes a malignancy to a benign tumor. Worry never prevents a car wreck involving someone you love. On and on it goes.

Jesus points out a similar futility: "And why do you worry about clothing?" That would make a great motto for The Gap—don't you think?

What worries are you carrying around? These words of Jesus aren't just for that little band gathered around the Sea of Galilee. They're words for everybody who seeks righteousness inside out. Notice how plain the words are. Worry is wrong. That makes worry a sin. It doesn't fit the life of one who believes that God is indeed ruling.

These words do not come, however, from a harsh judge who's looking for one more little corner where he can say, "Aha! Busted!" Rather, they're from one who loves his people and wants to free them from their fretting.

Conquering Worry

There are some decisions we have to make if we're going to overcome worry. While the power is with God, we (and, yes, I'm including myself!) have got to decide whether we're going to be eaten away by worry or not.

The first decision is to let God provide. If he takes such good care of the birds and flowers, surely he knows our needs and will care for us. He's a Creator to the flowers and the birds, but he's a Father to us.

Think about young children. Do they worry about eating? I'd venture to say my children never worried about eating. I don't think there's ever been a day that one of them wondered, "What if Mom or Dad don't fix any supper tonight?"

Jesus says that the pagans run after all these things. Note the aerobic quality of worry. They run, convinced that everything falls on their own shoulders. It's just as much pagan to worry about those things as it is to worship a false god.

But to his followers Jesus is saying, "What do you do with your worries?" Do you try to drink them away? Do you just stew in them? Do you keep putting all of them into your system so that eventually your body will just explode?

Turn all your worries over to God, Jesus invites us. Some of your worries are bigger than you are. The technological possibilities of what could happen to our future are much bigger than you, but they're not bigger than God. So Paul tells us: "Do not be anxious about anything, but in every situation, by prayer and petition, with thanksgiving, present your requests to God" (Phil. 4:6) Actually, God knows our concerns already. But he wants us to say, "Father, I have these concerns, and I'm giving them to you."

I know a man who got into an executive position that caused him to worry constantly over the financial solvency of his company. He began drinking heavily to sedate his nerves and escape. It was a classic case of taking a bad problem and making it worse. After he causes a wreck that killed someone, he realized that his central mistake was not turning those things over to God.

My scuba equipment provides air when I'm underwater, even though the tank is filled with air at a pressure of 3,000 pounds per square inch. There is so much air that if I open the valve completely, the blast could bowl someone over. It would be impossible to breath directly out of a tank. It would blow you up like a Macy's Parade balloon.

So a regulator attaches to the tank. The regulator's first stage takes the pressure from 3,000 to 100 pounds per square inch. Then its second stage, what I put in my mouth, gives me whatever air I need.

As I understand the promises of God, he doesn't tell us he'll remove all our pressures. Rather than promising to remove the burdens, he offers to be present with us and to help us bear them. In other words, it isn't so much the blessings of God that he offers as it is his presence.

Our second decision is to pursue God's rule. "But seek first his kingdom and his righteousness, and all these things will be given to you as well" (Matt. 6:33). Our calling isn't primarily to avoid bitterness, lust, dishonesty, and various vices. It's a positive calling to seek God, to find our joy in him, to listen to his voice, to find rest in his presence.

This passion for God and for his rule in our lives is echoed in this prayer which Soren Kierkegaard placed at both the beginning and end of his magnificent book *Purity of Heart Is to Will One Thing*:

> *Father in Heaven! What is man without Thee! What is all that he knows, vast accumulation though it be, but a chipped fragment if he does not know Thee! What is all his striving, could it even encompass the world, but a half-finished work if he does not know Thee; Thee the one, who are one thing and who are all! So may Thou give to the intellect, wisdom to comprehend that one thing; to the heart, sincerity to receive this understand-ing; to the will, purity that wills only one thing. In prosperity may thou grant perseverance to will one thing; amid distractions, collectedness to will one thing; in suffering, patience to will one thing. Oh, thou that giveth both the beginning and the completion, may Thou early, at the dawn of day, give to the young man the resolution to will one thing. As the day wanes, may Thou give to the old man a renewed remembrance of his first resolu-tion, that the first may be like the last, the last like the first, in possession of a life that has willed only one thing. Alas, but this has indeed not come to pass. Something*

has come in between. The separation of sin lies in between. Each day, and day after day something is being placed in between; delay, blockage, interruptions, delusion, corruption. So in this time of repentance may Thou give the courage once again to will one thing.

One Day At a Time

Finally, we have to decide to negotiate one day at a time. "Therefore do not worry about tomorrow, for tomorrow will worry about itself. Each day has enough trouble of its own" (Matt. 6:34).

One translation has "Take therefore no thought for the morrow." But that's not really what he was saying. He didn't mean that taking out an insurance policy or thinking about tomorrow is wrong. What he meant is, Don't worry about tomorrow. Precaution? Yes. Consideration about tomorrow? Yes. But don't worry about it. Just live one day at a time.

Sir William Osler put it well:

If the load of tomorrow be added to that of yesterday and carried today, it will make the strongest falter. Live in day-tight compartments. Don't let yesterday and tomorrow intrude on your life. Live one day at a time. You'll avoid the waste of energy, the mental distress, the nervous worries that dog the steps of the man who's anxious about the future.

I love this little statement Jesus makes at the end: "Each day has enough trouble of its own." What an optimistic note to end on! "Don't worry about tomorrow. You'll be lucky if you make it through today." I can see the deadpan look on his face as it starts to turn into a smile.

Toward the end of the movie "Butch Cassidy and the Sundance Kid," the two heroes are perched on a cliff.

They've been chased all over, and now they're finally out of running space. It's a long drop from this cliff down to the roaring river below. Sundance will not jump. Finally he confesses to Butch, "I can't swim." Just as they leap, Butch says, "Well, don't worry. The fall will probably kill you."

I love Shel Silverstein's poem entitled "Whatif." A child narrates, telling about some Whatifs that crawled inside his ears while he was lying in bed thinking. Some are a bit outlandish (typical for a child—or maybe for adults, too!): "Whatif there's poison in my cup?" "Whatif green hair grows on my chest?" "Whatif my head starts getting smaller?" Others are not so outlandish: "Whatif nobody likes me?" "Whatif they start a war?" "Whatif my parents get divorced?"[1]

Jesus knows that these "what if" games are completely unproductive. They can wreck a day and ruin a night. Why worry about tomorrow?

Right at the end of World War II, the Allies opened some camps for orphans. They worked hard to restore them to a sense of security. But in one particular camp, they experienced a problem. The children would not sleep. They'd put them to bed and turn out the lights, but the kids would not sleep even though they were physically exhausted. They couldn't. So the camp directors brought in some psychologists who recommended that every night before they tucked the children in, they put a piece of bread in the children's hands. Once they did that, immediately the kids began sleeping. Even though they had been well fed at these camps, their experience had taught them that there might be no food tomorrow. But with a piece of bread in their hands, they could go to sleep assured that when they woke up there would be something to eat.

What's that little piece of bread in your hand? Jesus said it's the knowledge that there is a Father who cares intimately and deeply about you. And when you go to bed at night, you have in the palm of your hand the assurance that God will never leave you or forsake you.

Chapter 13
SPECK INSPECTORS

Do not judge, or you too will be judged. For in the
same way you judge others, you will be judged, and
with the measure you use, it will be measured to you.
—Matthew 7:1

Several years ago, a church in Oklahoma excommunicated a woman for immorality. When she filed a lawsuit against the church, the story made all the national news media. And I'll never forget a friend's response when he shook with anger at that church: "Judge not that you be not judged!"

His righteous indignation well represented the spirit of our age—a spirit of compromise. While compromising is, in some contexts, essential, in other areas it refers to a mindset that will never evaluate, that disdains doctrine, conviction, confrontation, absolutes, and theology.

"Judge not that you be not judged" is parroted by people who have no earthly idea what Jesus means. I venture to say that the people who refer to this verse most are the ones who understand it the least. It just happens to fall into line with the spirit of this age.

A teenager is at odds with her parents because they

have laid down the rule that she can't go out with a certain boy because they think it would not be good for her spiritual development. So with her self-righteous nose turned upward, she storms out of the room and screams, "Judge not that you be not judged!" Slam goes the door. And she feels she's cleared her system of her responsibility to tell her parents off biblically.

Some student gets drunk and has to be disciplined on a Christian college campus. Immediately, his friends rally around and suddenly become "biblical," saying, "Judge not that you be not judged."

I had a friend in college who went to talk privately with two friends whom he was fairly certain were involved in a homosexual relationship. Of course they were offended that somebody would even think such a thing about them. So immediately they told all their friends. And who do you think became the bad guy? My friend, because he had done the one biblical thing. Instead of gossiping about it or writing letters to the editor, he went to them privately. Suddenly everyone was shouting to him, "Judge not that you be not judged!"

What was Jesus saying in Matthew 7? As I've said all along, the theme of the Sermon on the Mount is "Righteousness Inside Out," and the key verse in understanding it is Matthew 5:20. We must have a different kind of righteousness from that of the scribes and Pharisees. They wore theirs on their sleeves; it was superficial and ungodly.

Ours must grow out of a heart committed to the Father. Jesus' words now continue that theme, for he knew that the Pharisees were experts at judging others self-righteously.

Jesus said there are some problems with that kind of judging. One is that it's hypercritical, always going around with a censorious attitude, digging and searching for faults, always suspecting the worst. When you begin with yourself as the standard, everybody else looks pretty bad. It's a failure to exhibit the kingdom life of the first beatitude: poverty of spirit. When you feel you can stand on your own worth, that's when you start judging hypercritically.

Jesus wasn't saying we should never assess people with some discrimination, but rather that we should not have a harsh, judgmental spirit. John Stott put it this way: "Jesus does not tell us to cease to be men (by suspending our critical powers which help to distinguish us from animals) but to renounce the presumptuous ambition to be God (by setting ourselves up as judges)." That's what drives this hypercritical attitude: a belief that I can see as God sees. I can see your motives. I can see the way you're thinking. I know all the things that have led you in your spiritual pilgrimage to this point. That's what Jesus wants to eliminate.

Paul asked: "Who are you to judge someone else's servant? To their own master they stand or fall" (Rom. 14:4). I think of that verse every time a "religious" rag sheet comes to my attention, attacking other Christians unfairly. I also recall these words from the same apostle: "I care very little if I am judged by you or by any human court; indeed, I do not even judge myself. . . . It is the Lord who judges me. Therefore judge nothing before the appointed time; wait till the Lord comes" (1 Cor. 4:3f).

We can't know everything in everybody else's heart. I can't read all your motives. I can't see you as God does. I need to give you the benefit of the doubt. But above all, I shouldn't be going around trying to find faults in your life.

Notice that self-righteous judgment has a boomerang

effect. "For in the same way you judge others, you will be judged, and with the measure you use, it will be measured to you" (v. 2). In other words: "Look. If you start throwing out this censorious spirit on other people, it will come back and you'll be sorry."

But there's a second problem with Pharisaic right-eousness. Not only was it hypercritical, but it was also hypocritical. It was two-faced. We like to look at people with bifocals. We use the bottom part to see ourselves, and it tends to have a rosy tint to it, able to look past any shortcomings. But the top part with which we look out at others is jaundiced. And that's the hypocrisy he was denouncing.

Bertrand Russell capsulized this hypocrisy well in his emotive conjugations:

> I am firm.
> You are obstinate.
> He's pig-headed.
> I have re-considered.
> You have changed your mind.
> He's gone back on his word.

It's like the parable in Luke 18, where a Pharisee goes to the temple to pray. The Pharisee looks through the top part of his bifocals and says, "Oh my! I'm glad I'm not like that scumbag out there." Then he looks through the bottom part and says to God, "You are just so blessed to have me on your team." That's the kind of judging Jesus condemned.

Searching for Specks

Jesus' humorous side slips out in verse 3: "Why do you look at the speck of sawdust in your brother's eye and pay no attention to the plank in your own eye?"

We've heard it so many times that it has lost its humorous twist, but the people in Jesus' audience were likely chuckling. It sounds like a scene out of the Three Stooges. Here's one guy with a little piece of sawdust in his eye. There's somebody else with a two-by-four coming out of his forehead, and he's trying to get that speck of sawdust out. Every time he turns around, the other guy has to duck.

It's deadly to have somebody with a two-by-four in his eye trying to remove your piece of sawdust. And yet that's the very way we are. What is the two-by-four he was speaking about? It's not just a worse sin. It's self-righteousness, appointing yourself the official speck inspector of the church.

An illustration of that is found back in Genesis 38. Judah's daughter-in-law Tamar had lost her husband. Judah gave her another of his sons, but he wouldn't cooperate in giving her a child. Then he died and Judah wouldn't give her his youngest son as the law demanded. So Tamar did the only thing she could think of. When Judah announced he was going to the market, Tamar dressed as a prostitute, disguised herself, and seduced him, becoming pregnant in the process. Later, when Judah learned Tamar was pregnant out of wedlock, he demanded that she be burned to death.

So she walked out and said, "That's fine, but I want you to know that you are the father."

We can see so well the things in others' lives that displease us, but Jesus said we're usually hypercritical and hypocritical when we do it.

He didn't stop there, however. He didn't instruct us to stay out of other people's business. Rather, he gave us the responsibility of helping a fellow Christian by loving correction: "You hypocrite, first take the plank out of your own eye, and then you will see clearly to remove the speck from the other person's eye" (Matt. 7:5).

What is the loving, Christian thing to do when a friend comes to see you and she's got a speck in her eye? Turn and walk away? No! Tell her, "Oh, no. I could never take that out of your eye. I've had specks in my own eye before. I must get out of here"? Huh-uh! She's in pain. Refusing to help isn't the loving response.

Or suppose a child comes to you with a splinter in his finger. He's crying, "Please take this splinter out!" What's the Christian thing to do? Leave the splinter there? No! You take the splinter out. So Jesus was saying there is a place for some discernment in people's lives. If you see brothers or sisters who have specks in their eyes, you need to help them take it out!

But first you take the two-by-four of self-righteousness out of your own eye. Later in Matthew we read a fuller account of how this is to happen: "If a brother or sister sins, go and point out the fault, just between the two of you alone. If they listen to you, you have won them over. . . ." (Matt. 18:15). Paul put it this way: "Brothers and sisters, if someone is caught in a sin, you who live by the Spirit should restore that person gently" (Gal. 6:1).

You who are spiritual—not self-righteous—you who have evidence of fruit of the Spirit in your life, you go restore the person. Matthew 7:1 shouldn't interfere with the responsibility you have to go to somebody in loving confrontation.

Hogs and Dogs

Another responsibility Jesus didn't eliminate is discerning spiritual hogs and dogs. Verse 6 says, "Do not give dogs what is sacred; do not throw your pearls to pigs." If you think verses 1-5 prohibit any kind of discerning in judgment, you have a real problem here. You've got to use some kind of criteria to decide who those spiritual hogs and dogs are.

Jesus called things as he saw them. He saw the Pharisees and said, "Hi, you bunch of snakes." He saw Herod and said, "Oh, there's Herod the fox." And in Matthew 7 he is saying, "Now I want to talk to you about those people who are pigs and dogs."

"Don't give dogs what is sacred," Jesus said. We have a little trouble understanding that today, because our dogs are different from theirs. He wasn't talking about those cute little family members that wear rhine-stone collars and painted toenails. We had some friends in North Carolina who said their dog would not eat T-bone steak unless it was marinated properly and cooked medium rare. He wasn't talking about those kind of dogs. Instead, he was speaking of the flea-infested street mutts that don't care whether they have filet mignon or putrefied ox intestine. It makes no difference to them. Don't take filet mignon and throw it out to them; they'd just as soon have the other.

Don't give pearls to hogs either, because they're going to sniff them for a moment, trample on them, and then, to show their gratitude, turn around and tear you to shreds. You can take a pig and put him in a bathtub. You wash him. You floss his teeth. You put mousse on his tail. You do whatever you want. Then you put him back outside, and you know where he'll go? Right back to the mud. Jesus was saying there are people like that. These words sound harsh, but his point is that we should not waste spiritual treasures on those who have no spiritual interest.

My friend Randy Harris tells people that he remembers staying in our home years ago when our oldest was just four. We had pancakes for breakfast, with two kinds of syrup on the table: a treasured little bottle of Vermont maple syrup that I'd brought back from a trip and a large container of Aunt Jemima's. I passed him the Vermont syrup, then poured Aunt Jemima's on my son's pancakes. Randy says he looked at me quizzically and I explained, "Don't cast your pearl to swine." Assuming he remembers this story accurately, I was only referring to the inappropriateness of wasting something precious on someone who could not (yet!) appreciate it.

In Matthew 10 Jesus sends some people out, and he tells them not to waste their time in places where they aren't received. Instead, they are to "shake the dust from their feet" and move on. Some people are spiritual hogs and dogs.

Paul received some rough treatment in Corinth on his second missionary journey, and Luke reports:

> But when they opposed Paul and became abusive, he shook out his clothes in protest and said to them, "Your blood be on your own heads! I am innocent of it. From now on I will go to the Gentiles."
>
> Acts 18:6

We've got to use that kind of discernment and not waste spiritual treasures on people who will just trample them.

Now, this is the exception rather than the rule. We don't jump on this idea and stop evangelizing. But there are people who have no spiritual interest. They will trample the precious things we hold dear to our hearts. Jesus instructs us to use some discernment.

Do Unto Others

After the first six verses in Matthew 7, Jesus took a more positive approach. We all know his command in verse 12: "Do to others what you would have them do to you." Then he added, ". . . this sums up the Law and the Prophets."

Not surprisingly, this command is consistent with the character of God:

> *Ask and it will be given to you; seek and you will find, knock and the door will be opened to you. For everyone who asks receives; those who seek find; and to those who knock, the door will be opened.*
>
> *Which of you, if his son asks for bread, will give him a stone? Or if he asks for a fish, will give him a snake? If you, then, though you are evil, know how to give good gifts to your children, how much more will your Father in heaven give good gifts to those who ask him! So in everything, do to others what you would have them do to you, for this sums up the Law and the Prophets.*
>
> Matt. 7:7-12

The Jewish Talmud records a dialogue between a couple of rabbis, one named Hillel. Hillel made the statement, "What is hateful to you, do not do to anyone else." It's kind of a law of protection. But Jesus advanced beyond that thinking to put it positively. You be sure you do to other people the kind of things you want them to do to you.

A lot of people have piggy-backed on Christianity, trying to take this high ethic without the substructure of theology, recognizing that the reign of God has come near through the life, death, and resurrection of Jesus. But at least they've heard that command known as the Golden Rule.

Why Obey the Golden Rule?

Why should we live by the Golden Rule? The first reason is God's example. That's the way he is, and we've noticed elsewhere in the Sermon on the Mount that he's told us we ought to treat other people based on the way he treats them or the way he treats us.

So how does God treat us? Jesus said, "Ask and it will be given to you; seek and you will find." Then just start beating on the door, and somebody will open it. That's how God is: full of mercy and love.

Decades ago the mother of Marshall Field gave the University of Chicago a million dollars. Some people from the board of Northwestern University went to her and asked, "Why did you give them a million dollars but not us?"

The reply came back, "Because Northwestern did not ask for a million dollars."

Doors get opened when we knock and ask. That's the way it is with God too.

A child was going off to bed. He said to his family, "I'm going to be praying to God. Does anybody want anything?" That's a positive attitude that God is going to answer. Sometimes we pray thinking, "Well, I know he's not going to answer this anyway, but here goes." How much better it is to imitate that little boy!

I confess there are certain passages in the Bible that I wish weren't there, and this is one of them. So many people don't understand it. They go to all the passages like this, especially in the synoptic gospels, and suddenly come out thinking that God will grant every request they ever have. That leaves them with two directions they can go. One is to follow a path of self-deception where they really believe that's happening. The other is to conclude God has disappointed them.

God said, for example, that if you pray, you can move a mountain. So people conclude that if we pray, tomorrow there'll be no mountain. This unrealistic approach has destroyed a lot of people's faith.

So what did Jesus mean? You may have asked for things that weren't given. Maybe a life was not prolonged or a handicap wasn't healed. I don't know that I can answer all those questions, but I do know we have to rely on the goodness of God and the wisdom of God. John Stott's words are right on target: "Perhaps we would put the matter in this way: being good, our heavenly Father gives only good gifts to his children; being wise as well, he knows which gifts are good and which are not."

Those two qualities of God sit next to one another. He's good and he's wise, so he knows how to answer us. Verses 9-11 make that clear. A good parent doesn't agree to give his child a pet rattlesnake. Nor does he give the child who asks for a Pop Tart a tart pop in the nose. And God is the best parent there could be.

A second reason for obeying the Golden Rule is found at the end of verse 12. In addition to having God's example, we have God's consistent instruction. Jesus said: "For this sums up the Law and the Prophets." Later an expert in the Law would question Jesus: "Which is the greatest commandment in the Law?" Jesus' response helps us grasp the central themes of all God's instructions:

> *"Love the Lord your God with all your heart and with all your soul and with all your mind." This is the first and greatest commandment. And the second is like it: "Love your neighbor as yourself." All the Law and Prophets hang on these two commandments.*
>
> Matt. 22:37-40

Have you ever taken a bowl of Rice Krispies and crunched them down as much as you could? I have no idea why you would do that, but I remember having done it. You could take a full bowl and crunch it down, and then take it in a capsule form. You could fit the whole bowl in a capsule. You'd miss the snap, crackle, and pop, but you would have your cereal.

Jesus was saying that if you take the whole bowl of the Law and the Prophets and start crunching it down, compressing it, and putting it into one capsule, you would find that they were focused on love of God and love of others. Paul followed his Lord's understanding of scripture:

> Let no debt remain outstanding, except the continuing debt to love one another, for whoever loves others has fulfilled the law. The commandments, "Do not commit adultery," "Do not murder," "Do not steal," "Do not covet," and whatever other commandments there may be, are summed up in this one command: "Love your neighbor as yourself."
>
> Rom. 13:8f

What the Golden Rule is Not

Consider for a moment what the Golden Rule is not. It is not a law of preparation. "Do unto others *before* they do unto you." Have you ever lived that way? You know what a coworker is going to say about you, so you'll just get the jump on her and start some rumors about her. Out in the business world, isn't it well known that if you don't trample somebody, in a day's time he'll trample you? It's a ravenous world out there. People are all trying to climb to the top.

Jesus had the opportunity to live that way. In the

upper room on the night he was betrayed, he knew what Judas was going to do. He knew his time had come. Accordingly, he had the perfect opportunity to beat Judas to the punch. He could have raised a ruckus there and exposed Judas. But instead he washed all ten toes of that man who in just a moment would get up and betray him.

The Golden Rule is also not a law of reciprocation. If it were, it would read, "Do unto others *because* they did unto you." That's the way the Pharisees were living (Matt. 5:38). They had taken that eye-for-eye and tooth-for-tooth thought out of the Old Testament, stripped it from its context, and made it the rule for living. If somebody does something to you, that's the way you treat him. If someone does something nice to you, you do something nice for her. It's not all negative. But it's still not the way of God.

Third, the Golden Rule is not a law of manipulation: "Do unto others *so* they will do unto you." We're familiar with that approach, aren't we? If you want to get any place, you've got to lead people along the way you want to go. On the surface this looks like the Golden Rule, but it's got a hidden agenda. You're doing unto others not because that's the right way. You're doing unto them because you think you'll get something in return.

Jesus could have lived that way too. Satan tempted him, saying, "Jump off the temple. Let angels catch you." Surely that would have impressed the crowds— so much that they'd have been ready followers. Yes, Jesus could have lowered the demands of discipleship and manipulated everyone with that one great feat. But he didn't.

What the Golden Rule Is

Jesus calls us to treat others the way we think is right. Whether they ever treat us well doesn't matter. If you're getting ready to cheat somebody, you need to stop and ask the question, "Would I recommend this for the world?" If you're about to tell somebody a lie, would you recommend that kind of behavior for the whole world? Would you want that happening to you?

If you were beaten up, half naked, along the side of the road and somebody came walking up to you, what kind of behavior would you recommend?

If you were fourteen and pregnant, what kind of behavior would you recommend? Would you want others to flush with embarrassment every time they saw you? Or would you want them to love you unconditionally?

If you were homeless, what kind of recommendation would you give? How would you like to be treated? If you didn't have enough nutrition, how would you want to be treated? In one sense the Golden Rule calls us to social justice. We can't be oblivious to the needs of this world, because we're to treat people as we want to be treated.

Let's say gossip is circulating about somebody you don't like too well. What would you recommend? Just jump on the band wagon and keep it going? Maybe add a little bit to it? Well, how would you want somebody to treat you?

In marriage, do you want somebody to forgive you and put the past behind? Do you want somebody to have the eyes of Jesus and see your good qualities, focusing on them instead of your shortcomings?

Hillel said, "What is hateful to you, do not do to anyone else." Confucius said, "Whatever you do not want done to yourself, do not do to others." The Stoic slave-philosopher Epictetus said, "What you avoid suffering yourselves, seek not to inflict on others."

I guess we could all live by that negative rule. It protects us anyway. But that's not enough for Jesus. He is saying, "My love is active. It's not just saving your own skin by refraining from practices you don't want boomeranging on you. Whenever you see somebody, you have the opportunity to treat him the way God treats you. Do unto others as God has done unto you."

Chapter 14
TWO ROADS DIVERGE

Enter through the narrow gate. For wide is the gate and
broad is the road that leads to destruction, and many
enter through it. But small is the gate and narrow the
road that leads to life, and only a few find it.
—Matthew 7:13f

I've walked with friends through the Robert Frost paths in Vermont and New Hampshire. At one fork in the road, Frost's poem "The Road Not Taken" is posted. I keep a picture of that spot in my office to remind me of the two diverging roads that are always before me. For Frost was right: it makes all the difference which you choose!

Someone has wisely said that all of life concentrates on humanity at the crossroads. We live in the valley of decision. Before we go to bed at night, we decide what time to set the alarm clock for. In the morning, we decide whether to get up when it goes off or whether to smack the snooze button a few times. There's the decision of whether to have sausage with eggs for breakfast or left-over sausage pizza with Dr. Pepper.

Our day is filled with choices, for life is centered on decisions at the crossroads.

Some religious traditions tend to be nervous with much emphasis on human choice. "God is sovereign," they insist. Therefore everything that happens is just what God wanted to happen. If God knows that it's going to happen ahead of time, then it couldn't avoid happening.

Well, yes, God is indeed sovereign. But in his sovereignty, he chose to give us choice. He is interested in a true relationship, and real relationships demand that two sides be involved.

The Bible speaks often about the need to decide which way you're going to go. In Deuteronomy 30, Moses was wrapping up his time with the Israelites. He talked to them about all God had done and their many blessings. And then, as if he were singing his own invitation song, Moses called the people to make a choice.

> *This day I call heaven and earth as witnesses against you that I have set before you life and death, blessings and curses. Now choose life, so that you and your children may live and that you may love the Lord your God, listen to his voice and hold fast to him. For the Lord is your life, and he will give you many years in the land he swore to give your fathers, Abraham, Isaac and Jacob.*
>
> Deut. 30:19f

Years later, Joshua was wrapping up his time with the Israelites, and he also called them to make a decision. He reminded them of all God had done for them, and then he issued this challenge:

> *Now, fear the Lord and serve him with all faithfulness. Throw away the gods your forefathers worshiped beyond the River and in Egypt, and serve the Lord. But if serving the Lord seems undesirable to you, then choose for yourselves this day whom you will serve, whether the*

gods your forefathers served beyond the River, or the gods of the Amorites, in whose land you are living. But as for me and my household, we will serve the Lord.

Josh. 24:14f

The book of 1 Kings records a great contest on Carmel between the prophets of Baal and Elijah is recorded. Elijah challenged the bystanders, "How long will you waver between two opinions? If the Lord is God, follow him; but if Baal is God, follow him" (1 Kings 18:21). Again the crossroads. Pick one and go in that direction. This serious challenge runs all the way through the Bible.

In the Sermon on the Mount, Jesus has been calling us to a deeper righteousness—one that flows from penitent hearts responding to the rule of God. Now at the end, he calls for a decision. Two roads diverge . . . .

Two Gates and Two Roads

Jesus finishes the main body of his lesson in verse 12. The next verse begins the two options we now face. There are two gates. There are two roads. There are two animals. There are two trees, two fruits, and two destinies, and we've got to make a decision which one we're going to follow. Jesus didn't close wanting a bouquet of flowers for his efforts. Nor did he want applause for his high ethics or the approval of critics. Instead, he closed by demanding a decision. So we shouldn't come to the end of the Sermon on the Mount praising him for what he's said. Rather, we should come on our knees, deciding which way we'll go.

Consider those two gates. One is skinny, and one is broad. Naturally, the one that's narrow leads to the narrow road, and the broad one leads to the broad road. But what do they represent? Some have said they

177

represent those who are believers and those who are unbelievers. That interpretation could be true, but it's doubtful that was what he was talking about. Others have thought it pointed to one small sect that alone was honestly obedient to Christ. (Not surprisingly, they have generally thought it was *their* group!)

I believe, however, that the two roads are the two paths he has underscored all through the Sermon on the Mount. He isn't referring to believers and unbelievers but to the two kinds of people who claim to be in Jesus' camp. It's a very narrow road that holds the kind of people who walk by an inner righteousness. But there's a gigantic interstate highway full of people who walk with Pharisaic righteousness.

People on this broad road are saying, "Lord! Lord! Didn't we call on your name? Didn't we do things in your name?" That hardly describes unbelievers. The people on the broad road are the people who look like sheep on the outside but who are ravenous wolves on the inside. They stand in their own righteousness before God and say, "Lord, you are so lucky to have me on your side. I'm thankful I'm not like that sinner over there."

The narrow one holds those who are poor in spirit, who mourn, who are meek, who hunger and thirst for kingdom-shaped righteousness.

One road is like a main artery entering a city—wide, with many cars side by side. The other is like a little mountain road where two cars can't even pass. One of them has to back up to the last wide spot in the road. Jesus said most of the people are going to try to go on the pharisaic highway. It's only the select few who decide to let God take over. It's a serious choice we all make, because one of these roads goes to life, while the other leads to destruction.

Having told of the two gates and two roads in verses 13 and 14, Jesus now explains how to tell which of the two routes people have chosen. Watch for the two animals, the two trees, and the two fruits:

Watch out for false prophets. They come to you in sheep's clothing, but inwardly they are ferocious wolves. By their fruit you will recognize them. Do people pick grapes from thorn-bushes, or figs from thistles? Likewise, every good tree bears good fruit, but a bad tree bears bad fruit. A good tree cannot bear bad fruit, and a bad tree cannot bear good fruit. Every tree that does not bear good fruit is cut down and thrown into the fire. Thus, by their fruit you will recognize them.

Matt. 7:15-20

Sometimes we think it's easy to recognize false prophets. They're the ones who look like false prophets. But Jesus said that's not true, because false prophets dress up like true prophets. Spiritually they walk around saying, "Hey, we're sheep. We're with you. We're on your side."

Jesus said that only on the inside can you tell that the nose is a little longer than a sheep's nose, the teeth are a little sharper than sheep's teeth, and the ears are a little more pointed than sheep's ears. False prophets don't walk around with t-shirts saying, "I am a false prophet." That's why Jesus changed metaphors to say that by their fruit we will recognize them.

Calvin Miller tells of an antique wooden dynamite box with gigantic red and black letters that say, "DANGER! DYNAMITE!" But Miller wrote, "The last I saw it, it was filled with common paraphernalia that could be found in any workroom." And that's just what Jesus was talking about. False prophets may have signs

179

that say "DANGER! DYNAMITE!" as though they're on fire for the Lord. But you look inside and it's just the kind of stuff you've got in your attic.[1]

Another way to discern false prophets—those on the broad road—is to check the fruit of their lives. Suppose that last spring you planted a row of trees. You and your spouse are now arguing about whether you planted apple trees or peach trees. One sure way to settle the argument without calling in an expert is to wait until the trees have matured and see whether they bear apples or peaches.

If you go down one row in your garden and you can't remember later if you put in cucumbers or squash, wait a little. They look about the same at first, but it won't take long before you can tell whether it's squash or cucumbers.

The bad fruit has been mentioned throughout the sermon—judgmental attitudes, unwillingness to forgive, zealousness for earthly treasure, lust, etc.

Two Destinies

Next, Jesus spotlights the destinies of the people who choose the two roads:

> Not everyone who says to me, "Lord, Lord," will enter the kingdom of heaven, but only those who do the will of my Father who is in heaven. Many will say to me on that day, "Lord, Lord, did we not prophesy in your name and in your name drive out demons and in your name perform many miracles?" Then I will tell them plainly, "I never knew you. Away from me, you evildoers!"
>
> Matt. 7:21-23

The broad road people are the folks who have the godly appearance and know all the religious lingo. But

Two Roads Diverge

their hearts haven't been transformed. They may keep commandments like "Don't murder" and "Don't commit adultery" on the outside; but inside they are filled with bitterness and lust.

There are also the other people who are focused on God and want to do "the will of my Father." Notice that they *want* to do the will of the Father. They may not always do it perfectly, but that's what they want. That's what their lives are about. They want to do his will because they're in the relationship of child and father.

Have you been wavering between two opinions? It's time to choose between the two roads. One is broad, but it goes to destruction. The other is more narrow but it leads to life.

A Piece of the Rock

If you ever visit Stone Mountain outside of Atlanta, the guide will tell you it's 830 feet high. He will also probably tell you that it appears to be getting a little larger through the decades, because the storms come and erode the base of this mass of granite, exposing more of it. The rock actually seems to grow an inch every hundred years or so.

Jesus concluded the Sermon on the Mount by saying that if we put his words into practice we'll be like a wise man who built his house on the rock. And I think he knew—growing up in the home of his father, a carpenter—what he was speaking about when he discussed building houses. Maybe he was thinking, "I've built some condos on the Sea of Galilee. They just don't last. But I've also built some houses right here on some of these rocks, and they last."

The difference between the two houses Jesus describes is subtle. A lot of people would think they were exactly the same. For one thing, the houses look alike. As far as we know, they may have been built from the same blueprint. The windows look the same. The structure is about the same. The garages, the doors, the color—all are alike.

In the same way, you can look at two people who are about the same height and nearly the same weight. Both look to be athletic. They may also appear to be equally healthy. But suppose that on the inside one man's body is eaten up with a disease. Outwardly the two look the same. But inwardly they're not.

Jesus says the difference between a false prophet and a true disciple is going to be subtle, because they look about the same. Both of them look like sheep, but only one really is a sheep. Both of them fast. Both of they pray. Both give alms. Both go to church. Both have religious literature sitting out on the dining room table. Both have Bibles stacked in their cabinets. Neither is a murderer. Neither commits adultery. Neither tells out-and-out lies. Both profess to be disciples.

One man built his house on a rock, and the other man built his house on sand. And the one who builds on a solid, stable rock foundation is the person who takes Jesus' words and does them. What words are those? The words he's been talking about all the way through—words that call us to an inner righteousness where God is in control.

If you don't do that, Jesus says, if you just listen to these words and never act on them, you're building on sand. It's skin-deep righteousness. It's the righteousness that lacks punch. It's the kind of righteousness that keeps only enough rules to stay out of trouble, while never really wanting to keep the rules at all.

The Choice

Jesus said storms are going to come into every life. A loved one may suffer or die. A job may be lost. A relationship may be torn apart. And when storms like that come, a Pharisaic righteousness can't carry you. It may last through the calm all right, but not through the storm.

These storms are going to come in your life, though I can't predict exactly what form they'll take. The rain will come. The streams will rise. The wind is going to blow, and it will beat against your house. And whether your house of faith stands or falls depends on where you have built.

Soren Kierkegaard told a parable of ducks gathering for duck church. They waddled into their duck pews, sang from their duck hymnals, listened to their duck preacher whose sermon was probably recorded on duck tape. (All right, I'm adding a bit!) The duck preacher said, "Ducks, you don't have to waddle. You have wings like eagles. You can fly! Fly, ducks, fly!" The ducks replied, "Amen! Amen!" Then when the service was over, Kierkegaard said, the ducks got up and waddled home.

This is a fitting description of those who contemplate righteousness, who think about giving themselves to God—but who never go beyond the "thinking about" stage.

God longs to turn our world upside down. But for that to happen through us, we must allow him to turn us inside out. Where have you been building: on the sand of externals or the rock of righteousness inside out? The power is God's. He is the one who can radically change you.

But the choice is yours.

ENDNOTES

Chapter 1

1. Dallas Willard, *The Divine Conspiracy* (San Francisco, CA: HarperCollins, 1998), 134.

Chapter 2

1. We should keep in mind that not all Pharisees were like those condemned in Matthew. Their roots went back at least to the Maccabean revolt when law-observing Jews reacted against the infiltration of Hellenistic influence. They stand as a reminder of how a good, well-intentioned movement can get off track.

2. To go deeper into studies of the social world behind the writing of Matthew's gospel, refer to J. Andrew Overman, *Matthew's Gospel and Formative Judaism* (Minneapolis: Fortress, 1990) and the background section in Craig Keener's masterful and exhaustive work, *A Commentary on the Gospel of Matthew* (Grand Rapids: Eerdmans, 1999). Keener writes, "I find in the Gospel an author and audience intensely committed to their heritage in Judaism while struggling with those they believe to

be its illegitimate spokespersons. On this reading, Matthew writes to Jewish Christians who, in addition to being part of their assemblies as believers in Jesus, are fighting to remain part of their local synagogue communities" (p. 49).

3. This story is found in Matthew 15.

4. Willard, *The Divine Conspiracy*, 142f.

Chapter 3

1. Willard, *The Divine Conspiracy*, 150.

2. "Fools say in their hearts, 'There is no God.' They are corrupt, and their ways are vile" (Psalm 53:1). "As a dog returns to its vomit, so fools repeat their folly" (Proverbs 26:11). See many similar passages in the Wisdom Literature of the Old Testament.

Chapter 4

1. J. R. R. Tolkien, *The Hobbit*.

2. Richard Hays, *The Moral Vision of the New Testament* (San Francisco, CA: HarperCollins, 1996), 401.

Chapter 5

1. Richard Hays, *The Moral Vision of the New Testament* (San Francisco, CA: HarperCollins, 1996), 347f.

2. For an insightful look at the "redemptive movement" in scripture in its treatment of women, see William Webb, *Slaves, Women & Homosexuals* (Downer's Grove, IL: InterVarsity, 2001)

3. Two excellent resources for looking at the intricate

difficulties involved in divorce and remarriage are Richard Hays, *The Moral Vision of the New Testament*, pp. 347-378 and Craig Keener, *And Marries Another* (Peabody, MA: Hendrickson, 1991).

4. Walter Wangerin, *As For Me and My House* (Nashville, TN: Thomas Nelson, 1987), 79

Chapter 6

1. James Patterson and Peter Kim, *The Day America Told the Truth* (New York: Prentice Hall, 1991), 45.

Chapter 8

1. Frederick Buechner, *The Magnificent Defeat* (San Francisco, CA: Harper & Row, 1966), 105. Used by Permission.

Chapter 9

1. Henri Nouwen, *The Inner Voice of Love* (New York: Doubleday, 1996), 5.

2. Willard, *The Divine Conspiracy*, 191.

3. John Stott, *The Message of the Sermon on the Mount* (Downers Grove, IL: InterVarsity, 1978), 129.

4. This teaching was based on a mistaken under-standing of God's kingdom. Believing the terms "kingdom" and "church" were synonymous— which it now seems clear to me that they're not— the leaders taught that we should no longer pray for the kingdom to come since the church has been established.

5. Willard, *The Divine Conspiracy*, 195.

Chapter 10

1. From Lewis Smedes, *Forgive and Forget* (San Francisco, CA: Harper & Row, 1984), xiii-xv. Used by permission. The material from this excellent book was very helpful in writing this chapter.

2. Ibid., 126f.

Chapter 12

1. Shel Silverstein, *A Light in the Attic* (New York: Harper & Row, 1981), 90

Chapter 14

1. From Gordon MacDonald, *Restoring Your Spiritual Passion* (Nashville, TN: Thomas Nelson, 1986), 205.